T0167157

A Journey through Life
with
Don Hamacher,
Cofounder of
DOG n SUDS

A Memoir by

Don Hamacher

iUniverse, Inc.
Bloomington

A Journey through Life with Don Hamacher, Cofounder of Dog N Suds

Copyright © 2012 Donald Ralph Hamacher

iUniverse books may be ordered through booksellers or by contacting:

iUniverse
1663 Liberty Drive
Bloomington, IN 47403
www.iuniverse.com
1-800-Authors (1-800-288-4677)

ISBN: 978-1-4759-3184-6 (sc)
ISBN: 978-1-4759-3186-0 (hc)
ISBN: 978-1-4759-3185-3 (e)

Library of Congress Control Number: 2012910096

Printed in the United States of America

iUniverse rev. date: 6/25/2012

This book of memories is dedicated to our loyal Dog N Suds family and franchisees, my own family, and many friends who have made my life so special.

Contents

THE PREFACE:
A Promising Beginning

Perhaps I was flattered by the fact that someone from years gone by had actually read *The History of The Long Bay Symphony* that I had written. This commissioned commemorative book honoring the prestigious orchestra born and nourished in the Myrtle Beach, South Carolina area offered a wealth of information to only those who had contributed that wealth of information in the first place. The Board of Directors, the founders, the women's guild—to name a few involved parties. After publication of this time-consuming assignment, the silence was deafening. Imagine my astonishment when a friend of the Symphony called on behalf of a fellow board member who asked if I would be interested in writing his life story. My friend added that the gentleman is ninety years old, has been married to the same lucky woman, Maggie, for sixty-seven years and is waiting for my reply. Further instructions from my somewhat pushy, lovable friend were to call him a.s.a.p. I obeyed her command immediately. I was curious to say the least.

Of great importance here is some significant personal background information to explain my immediate acceptance of this enormous challenge. My mother must have rocked me to sleep singing the musical score from *Oklahoma!* with emphasis on the lyrics of "I'm Just the Girl Who Cain't Say No". The second line of this lilting melody is "…and I'm in a turrible fix." Those words should have influenced big time my decision to take on this task of retelling Donald Hamacher's life story. I tried to think of logical reasons and defensible excuses to turn my back on his request for my writing services. Additional factors influenced my decision. I consulted my trusty writing friends who oohed and aahed about how interesting, intriguing, and challenging this project would be. They can be very persuasive but the bottom line was that I have never learned to say NO and should be in therapy for this condition.

So on a rather chilly winter afternoon with legal pad and pen in hand, I am seated comfortably at one end of a cozy flowered sofa in a lovely North Myrtle Beach home. Nestled at the other end sat Mr. Don Hamacher, tall, smiling, bright-eyed in a very Ralph Lauren-type plaid shirt, and to top it off he is crowned with a full head of wavy salt and pepper hair. Clearly my subject is not the stereotypical nonagenarian. Immediately I like what I see and I hope the feeling is mutual. To the gentleman's right stands a bookcase filled with dozens and dozens of stuffed photo albums with intimidating large-printed titles: THE DOG n SUDS STORY, CHINA, EGYPT, AFRICA, PANAMA CANAL, TURKEY, ALASKA. This long-married couple are travelers without boundaries. Below those tomes are more shelves of chronologically arranged albums fraught with articles, pictures, and commentaries covering Don's long life of accomplishments and experiences. I am astonished to learn that he is a founder of DOG n SUDS and am anxious to discover the details of his ninety-one well-lived years.

Don, on the other hand, is most anxious to start at the beginning, pulls the first volume from his life shelves. I listened attentively to his narration as he turns the pages with pride. I soon realize I am in the presence of a man who had been a musician, a teacher, a former drum major, a dance band leader, a high school band director, an eagle scout and beyond, an organizer of singers, a singer himself, a patron of the arts, a performer, a Sunday school class teacher and choir director, a traveler, a businessman and entrepreneur, a risk-taker, a pilot, an historian, a thinker, and a wonderful story teller. He relates the account of the two carat diamond he had chosen for his lovely wife for their twenty-fifth wedding anniversary. At the time he wanted the presentation to be special so he flew her in his twin engine airplane to the island of Eleuthera near the Bahamas. (He had once owned six planes and had logged 6,000 plus hours and added that he had stopped counting airtime at that point). While the happy couple was sitting on the beach, he dug into the pink sand and said, "What's this I found here?" At that point he placed the dazzling gem that he discovered buried on that beach on the finger of his beautiful smiling wife. Add 'romantic' to his many virtues and talents. This remarkable gentleman has "done it all" with zest, passion, and dignity and now he wanted me to document his story. That initial afternoon meeting wore on and my mind wore down. How does one approach this intriguing assignment? Think fast, come up with a decision and a plan quickly. Don Hamacher is a man of action, does not take No for an answer, and wants to get started.

My turn to contribute some brilliance to this first encounter. From some mysterious corner of the cerebrum emerges a possible plan of attack. I stare at the bookcase filled with the thick,heavy books. The chronicles of his rich life were there filled with resources and research. The Don Hamacher Memories Library stood very straight, side-by-side on the sturdy shelves begging to be of service. He listens as I explain what we could accomplish together in this portrayal of his amazing life. We can focus on each phase, accomplishment, experience he had enjoyed, recall decisions he had made, include the people who influenced and helped him along the way. We should retell the highs and lows of some ventures, the memorable moments, the love of his family, the important steps he made in life, obstacles he faced, and most interesting of all, things he wished he had done or hadn't done. Lessons learned and the passing on of that accumulated wisdom would prove invaluable to the next generation. I state my proposal and, in the long, deafening silence that follows, I wait patiently for some sign of approval or rejection.

At last he leans his head back on the pillowed sofa, places his hand on his steady forehead, remains quiet for a while. Then he sits up straight, sighs, and says, "I think I see what you mean." I recognize that this is the way Don Hamacher indicates agreement with the plans made by others. I begin to breathe again and as predicted the "girl who cain't say no" decides to commit to the project. The die is cast so next Saturday (and many Wednesdays and Saturdays after that), we sit again on his comfortable flowered sofa and try to uncover one golden treasure at a time. The retelling of Donald Hamacher's journey through life begins.

Gail Ritrievi
January 2011

DONALD R. HAMACHER

CHAPTER ONE:
Don's Early Life and Father's Influence

September 7, 1920 was certainly a groundbreaking date for Ralph and Lydia Hamacher. Their family expanded for the fourth time but after welcoming three beautiful daughters into their happy circle, a brave little male entered the picture. Donald Ralph Hamacher burst on the scene and they could not have been happier.

Don, in his own words, explains:" *How do I know they were thrilled with their boy, you may ask? I have pages in my extensive collection of photo albums that clearly show the love and pride in my parents' eyes and smiles as they held their baby boy for his many camera sessions. I modestly admit that I immediately became the major focus of my parents and sisters' attention. Now in 2011, if you have done the math correctly, you have deduced that I am heartily enjoying the ninety-first year of a wonderful life filled with love, happiness and adventure. I'm sorry that I only got to enjoy my mother's love and care for six years. She died in 1926.*

My father and his wisdom most especially guided me toward living an honorable life. Although he died in 1954 his words continue to resound in my mind and heart. I recall when I was a senior in high school my father and I had a very important discussion about life.

(This parental rite is often referred to as "The Talk".) I still hear his voice: "From birth until you die, that's your time on earth. What you contribute while you're here, that's important. Your reputation will carry you—protect it well. Always hold your head up high. Live by the Boy Scout oath. Just remember—Do your best. You don't always have to win to be successful in everything you do. And remember that your mother was a lady." I certainly understood that his words of wisdom meant that I should always be an honorable person.

When my father asked what I wanted to study in college, I revealed that my main choice was music, my first love. From my childhood I can still recall the contentment I felt sitting next to my father at many church choir practices. As my sisters and I grew old enough we sang in that choir every Sunday with my mother as the organist. My father planted the seed that nourished my love for all things musical and I am grateful to him and my family for that. I must add that after the declaration of my desired career choice, he looked me straight in the eyes and very seriously stated, "Music is a wonderful avocation but you may want to have another field of study as your life work." As usual he was right, but I was not easily convinced.

Inspired by the experience with a summer school instrumental program when I was in the seventh grade, I discovered the wonders of the clarinet. This enabled me to play other reeds just by adjusting the lip which was a challenge but great fun as well. I played in the high school band, and was the drum major in my junior and senior years. Given the opportunity to lead the concert band when the director was out of town or at meetings, I found another benefit in my passion for all things lyrical. Soon I formed a six piece dance band with my friend Don Jackson, our lead trumpet. We played at dance halls in towns close by and earned $35.00 for three hours which broke down to $5.00 each and $5.00 for expenses. In the summer of our senior year we played every Friday and Saturday nights at Lake Maurer. For that job we became a nine piece band. We were hot as they say nowadays. In the meantime I became interested in scouting.

2

RICHMOND HIGH SCHOOL BAND
DON WAS DRUM MAJOR TWO YEARS

1937 - 1938

CHAPTER TWO:
All Boys Should be Scouts

"On my honor I will do my best to do my duty to God and my country and to obey the scout law. To help other people at all times. To keep myself physically strong, mentally awake and morally straight." This is the oath that Don Hamacher repeated many times throughout his scouting years in Troop #324 in Richmond, Missouri and can still recite with pride and enthusiasm those words he lives by throughout his honorable life.

He went from Tenderfoot to Eagle Scout that required twenty-one merit badges. He proceeded to earn six Palms—Bronze, Gold and Silver. Each Palm required five additional merit badges Don earned 84 merit badges in all. There were only three other known scouts that had received that many.The most difficult for him was the Lifesaving badge since he claims he was more a farm boy than a swimmer. He cannot stress enough his deep feeling that scouting is a must for a boy. The laws alone are strong guidelines: A scout is trustworthy, loyal, helpful, friendly, courteous, kind, obedient, cheerful, thrifty, brave, clean, and reverent. These are characteristics everyone should possess.

Don's mentor in his scouting days was Roe Bartel, the chief scout executive and a former mayor of Kansas City. a president of Rotary Clubs International and a terrific inspirational speaker. Roe's father was a Presbyterian minister who lived across the street from the Hamacher family in Richmond, Missouri and talked with the young Don a great deal. His cousin Oliver Buchanan was an Eagle scout and taught him camping skills. Don's father was a miller and processed and sold flour, cornmeal, and grains to stores in town. Don was a natural pitchman and even helped deliver the many orders he sold to the merchants in town. His father also owned a farm eight miles south of Richmond, Missouri that the Littleman family managed. Don spent a summer working on his farm merit badges – dairying, farm mechanics and farm layout. There was no idle time for the Hamacher boy.

Don's motivating factor for choosing a college was whether there was an opening in the school's dance band. Don found a job at Kansas State-Emporia with the Lee Johnson band. Toward the end of the first semester Roe Bartel, who marveled at Don's scouting achievements, contacted Don that he found him a full scholarship opportunity at Northwest Missouri State Teachers College. The job would be to find merit badge examiners for the Boy Scouts. The Chamber of Commerce would help find qualified community people competent in their respective fields related to the merit badge requirements. While there, Don played oboe in the orchestra and saxophone in Tiger Pool's dance band. He always kept active with music throughout his scouting career.

The following year, Don found a spot at Missouri University. While there he established Alpha Phi Omega, a scouting fraternity for the purpose of meeting and continuing the positive influence of the Boy Scouts of America.

Life was good. He was playing with the Eddie Gibbon's dance

band, booking other bands to play sorority and fraternity dances and making his way through college. A few years later after Don was married and in his first teaching job, Roe Bartel appeared again to offer him the Boy Scout Executive Director position at Champaign, Illinois. The glitch in that opportunity was that Don would have to raise his own salary with fund-raisers. (This was before the United Fund helped support non-profit organizations.) Of course Don was flattered by the honor of being considered, but felt like he had to refuse that offer.

Thus ended Don's scouting connections. Although later in 1960, he headed a Boy Scout fund drive in Champaign, Illinois and in 1965 he appeared on the national television show "One In A Million". He was in his full scouting attire and demonstrated how to start a fire with flint and steel in 10 seconds. Scouting had a strong influence on Don's life keeping him physically strong, mentally awake and morally straight.

SECOND SILVER PALM

BY 1939- DON HAD RECEIVED HIS
SECOND SILVER PALM AWARD
ABOVE THE EAGLE- AND EARNED
84 MERIT BADGES. AT THAT TIME
THERE WERE ONLY 2 SCOUTS IN
THE U. S. WITH MORE MERIT
BADGES.

6O YEARS LATER-DON IS IN UNIFORM
SHOWING HIS AWARDS TO LOCAL
SCOUTS IN NORTH MYRTLE BEACH

CHAPTER THREE:
College, Meeting Maggie and Marriage

The narration of these momentous occasions should be given in Don Hamacher's words. *At Kansas State College in Emporia I landed a job with Lee Johnson's band that had just won the prestigious Battle of Bands in Kansas City. My next collegiate step was Missouri State Teachers College where I did mentor recruiting work for the Boy Scouts. Here I managed to play oboe in the college concert orchestra and played weekend nights with Tiger Pool's band. I realized that I could put myself through school, make some extra money for living and enjoy every minute of it. Finally my goal of studying music at Missouri University was made possible and I was thrilled at the chance to transfer. It is hard to believe but after my first year there, I was asked to become the drum major of the Missouri University marching band. Always the ambitious one, I played nights with the popular Eddie Gibbons dance band and began to book the other two bands for fraternity/sorority parties and for a 10% booking fee. I was rich—sort of. All this happened during World War II and I was able to stay in school by participating in the Marine Reserve Program. I had been there about a year when I met Maggie.*

Meeting Maggie was like a story book itself. Missouri Univ. had just

won the big 6 footbal lChampionship and we all walked out of class for a
pep meeting. I had a Spanish class with Gloria Hunter, Maggie's sister,
and as we were walking out of class together Maggie appears. Of course,
Gloria introduces her to me. About that time the University President
spoke on the P.A. system and warned us to return to our classes or receive
a negative hour. I told Maggie that I had seen her before and had wanted
to meet her. Then, I told her that I would like to take her across the street
to Gablers for a coke after class. Her answer was "If you see me after
class." I sensed that she really didn't want to go, and that she would try to
slip out the back way. She did just that and I was there waiting for her.
She was a good sport and went with me to Gablers for a coke. We had a
good time laughing and talking for about an hour, when she looked at her
watch and said that she had to go and that she was really running late.
We went outside and there was a taxi sitting there. I said let's get in and
we will get you home in nothing flat. Now I had never been in a taxi in
my life. On the way back to her hall, I shocked her to death when I said
",you know you're just the girl that I've been looking for and I'm going to
marry you." She just laughed and said "you're funny." After I got back to
my fraternity house, I did something else that I'd never done before. I sent
her a dozen roses. By this time she must have thought I was crazy and I
was — crazy over her. I let things cool off for a week then I called her for
another coke date. We enjoyed doing that for a few times. Then we started
studying together at the library. On Sundays, we would go to church
together, have lunch, then take a walk in the park and maybe take a picnic
supper. I often invited her to my fraternity house for dinner. She really
enjoyed visiting with our house mother, Mrs. Miller. Later on that year
I pinned her as my Phi Delta Theta Sweetheart. Maggie was a beautiful
girl. Every time there was a queen contest, they would choose her to be a
contestant. Her freshman year she was crowned Barn Warming Queen.
Then in 1943 she was selected a Savitor Yearbook Queen. Soon after that

we were engaged to be married . I graduated that year in June with a Bachelor's degree in Music.

After graduation I reported to Paris Island for Marine boot camp, then on to Quantico where they discovered my eyesight did not qualify me for further Marine service. I was honorably discharged and sent home with mixed feelings. I had always dreamed of becoming a Marine band director. On the way home I visited the Bernie Cummings dance band in St. Louis,Mo. While there, I was able to land a job playing with them. We played in such places as the Hotel New Yorker, the Aragon in Chicago and the Blue Moon in Witchita for about six weeks. Then we landed a contract at the Brown Hotel in Louisville,Ky. All this time Maggie and I had stayed in contact with each other. She kept reminding me that we should not get married until I found a steady job, not with a dance band. I guess I really lucked out when one of the members of the band told me that the high school music position was going to be open in January in his home town, Robinson, Ill. I jumped at the chance and called the Superintendent of schools at Robinson. He asked me to meet him in Indianapolis for an interview. I met him and he gave me the job. Maggie came down to Louisville the next weekend and we made our wedding plans. We were married on January 2, 1944 at the Methodist church in her home town, Paris, Missouri. We went to the Edge Water Beach Hotel in Chicago for our honeymoon. That was a beautiful experience. At that time I beleve it was one of the top hotels in the countrty. After that we went to Robinson, Ill. to start our married life and my music career.

MISSOURI UNIVERSITY
MY SENIOR YEAR -- 1942 - 1943

-- SCHOOL COURSES THAT I NEEDED WERE AVAILABLE AND OFERED AT CONVIENT TIMES.
-- PLAYED IN THE EDDIE GIBBONS DANCE BAND WITH THE MEAL JOB.
-- CREATED A NEW JOB ----- STARTED BOOKING THE TWO COLLEGE UNION DANDS TO PLAY FOR THE SORORITY & FRATERNITY DANCES. AT $10.00 PER DANCE, THAT NETTED $40.00 MOST WEEKS.
- ANOTHER GREAT THING HAPPENED-----THE UNION ALLOWED ME TO BOOK NON UNION BANDS, IF AND WHEN OUR UNION BANDS WERE ALREADY BOOKED. A LOCAL BLACK BAND WAS EAGER TO START PLAYING DANCES ON THE CAMPUS, AND THEY GAVE ME $50.00 PER DANCE TO BOOK THEM.-- WOW -- THAT ALONE NETTED ME $100.00 ON MANY WEEKS. I ENJOYED THAT SITUATION THRU MY JUNION & SENIOR YEARS. YES, I MADE $150.00 ON MANY WEEKS. THIS WAS QUITE A CONTRAST TO MY 1st TEACHING JOB AT $150.00 PER MONTH.
-- PLEDGED PHI DELTA THETA FRATERNITY AND MOVED INTO THE HOUSE.
-- BECAME DRUM MAJOR OF THE MISSOURI UNIVERSITY BAND DURING SECOND SEMESTER -- STRICTLY MILITARY -- NO BAND SHOWS.

EDDIE GIBBON'S DANCE BAND

DON PLAYED LEAD SAX WITH THIS BAND
WHILE HE WAS AT MISSOURI UNIVERSITY

MARGARET'S COLLEGE YEARS
A BARNWARNING QUEEN

MISSOURI
UNIVERSITY

1941 - 1942

DON ASKED MARGARET TO WEAR
HIS PHI DELTA THETA PIN

THE BARNWARMING QUEENS
MARGARET ON THE LEFT

MARGARET HAD AN EXCITING TWO AND A HALF YEARS HERE ON THE CAMPUS,
SHE ARRIVED HERE IN THE FALL OF 1941 -- LIVED AT HENDRIX HALL WHERE HER
SISTER, GLORIA, LIVED. THEY WERE BOTH OUTSTANDING STUDENTS -- SOCIALLY
SCHOLASTICALLY. MARGARET, HER FIRST SEMESTER, WAS SELECTED A
BARN-WARMING QUEEN . HER SISTER HAD BEEN AN ENGENEERING QUEEN IN 1940.
MARGARET WAS INTERESTED IN WORKING FOR A DEGREE IN PHYSICAL EDUCATION &
DRAMATICS -- HAD SHE HAD TIME TO FINNISH. SHE WAS VERY POPULAR AT HENDRIX HALL,
AND OUTSIDIE OF STUDYING - SHE AND HER GIRL FRIENDS HAD A LOT OF FUN DOING CRAZY
THINGS. SOON AFTER FOOTBALL SEAEON - SHE MET DON WHO WAS A JUNIOR IN THE SCHOOL OF
MUSIC AND A MEMBER OF THE PHI DELTA THETA FRATERNITY. THAT FRIENDSHIP DEVELOPED
QUITE RAPIDLY. IN FACT, IN THE SPRING, DON PINNED HER HIS PHI DELTA THETA
SWEETHEART. AFTER THAT - ALL THE PHI DELTS ADOPTED MARGARET AS THEIR QUEEN
DON & MARGARET STUDIED SOME TOGETHER MOST EVERYDAY & ALWAYS WENT TO CHURCH
TOGETHER ON SUNDAYS -- THEN WENT HIKING. ON SUNDAY AFTERNOONS. DON PLAYED IN
DANCE BANDS MOS EVERY NIGHT. LATER THAT SPRING SAM COOK, A PHI DELT BROTHJER,
INVETED SEVERAL COUPLES FOR A DAY OF FUN AT HIS FATHER'S SUMMER PLACE DOWN
ON THE LAKE OF THE OZARKS -- WHAT A DAY--

13

MARGARET'S COLLEGE YEARS

MARGARET'S SOPHOMORE YEAR CONTINUED TO BE EXCITING. SHE MAINTAINED HER HIGH SCHOLASTIC RECORDS AS WELL AS HER POPULARITY. THE THRILL OF HER BEING SELECTED A BARNWARMING QUEEN LAST YEAR WAS EXCEEDED BY HER BEING SELECTED AS ONE OF THE YEAR BOOK SAVITOR QUEENS THIS YEAR. TO TOP THAT --- LATER ON THAT SEMESTER --- DON GAVE HER AN ENGAGEMENT RING. THEY PLANNED TO GET MARRIED WHEN DON GOT OUT OF THE MARINES.

MARGARET HUNTER
SAVITOR QUEEN

DON'S HOME
FROM THE MARINES

BRIDE AND GROOM

DON AND MARGARET WERE MARRIED
JANUARY 2,. 1944

CHAPTER FOUR:
Don's Music Career — Robinson
— Macmurray — Champaign

My music career started at Robinson, Illinois High School in January, 1944. The Robinson Music Department had a fine reputation throughout that area. The quality of the students was exceptional, all eager and willing to follow my leadership and innovative ideas. Of course they wanted me to organize a dance band at once. It would consist of five brass, five saxophones and three rhythms. They suggested that we try to find a job playing at a summer resort. I agreed to take them if they found such a job and if we were able to develop a band capable of holding a summer job. Believe it or not, they found a job in less than a week and we were asked to come for an interview. The job was at Indiana Beach close to Indianapolis. They liked our band and we were hired. We had a fine high school band the rest of that school year and we attended several contests with much success. During one of the contests, I heard a trombonist play his solo. He was outstanding and I knew we should have him play with us at Indiana Beach. I contacted him and his parents and he was very happy that they let him go with us. We featured him all summer. I might add that he, Bob Burgess, later on joined the Stan Kenton Orchestra in the late forties.

We all enjoyed the job at Indiana Beach for ten weeks that summer. About the middle of the summer, our lead trumpet started failing on the high notes. (His lip was burnt out.) We had to do something quick. The manager suggested that we find a professional trumpet player to play lead, and move the lead trumpet to 2nd, our 2nd to 3rd, and send the 3rd home. We did find a good lead trumpet. At the same time we found a way to keep our original 3rd trumpet player with us by letting him share the 3rd part. We did this by letting one of them play before the intermission and the other one after the intermission. In the meantime, Maggie saw an ad in a magazine for pistols that shot nickels as the ammunition. We dreamed up the idea of starting a pistol shooting stand in front of the dance hall. We used the pistols to shoot nickels at packages of cigarettes sitting on a shelf. If the person shooting the nickels knocked the cigarettes off the shelf, they would get to keep the cigarettes. The two 3rd trumpet players took turns operating the stand before and after the intermission. This venture paid off well. It netted us ten times the additional cost of the professional lead trumpet. The summer was a wonderful experience for the students And it showed up in the quality of our high school band the following season.

The people of Robinson took us right in and treated us royally. Jim and Erma Biehl found us an apartment and they later became our close friends. The Hoods and the Nunnilees, who were high school athletic fans, introduced us to their group of friends. Dr Walt Schmidt and his wife Gin, adopted us. They found us a car, paid our way into the Robinson Country Club and loaned us the money to buy a home. Our married life started out well.

During Christmas vacation, while visiting Maggie's folks in Sedalia, Mo. Dr Hunter introduced me to a man who owned a Sunny Cal. bottling franchise. He distributed bottled fruit drinks to grocery stores. I thought this was a great idea, so I purchased the franchise for the city of Terre Haute Indiana, forty miles from Robinson, rented a building, purchased a truck and was in business in no time. I hired two young men to run the business while I continued with my music position in Robinson. The next summer, I was offered the franchise for Indianapolis, Indiana. That immediately increased the value of the business and I sold it for a profit and continued with my music career.

While at Robinson High School for 6 ½ years, our music department won the State Crown for two consecutive years. This award was won by the school that racked up the most points at the State contest. A band, choir or orchester received 20 points, an ensemble 10 points, and a solo.5 points for a first division. We racked up over 100 points both of those years.

Another interesting program that we originated was Musical Moods, a variety show consisting of three different moods, a religious mood, a variety show and a popular mood. This show appealed to all tastes, and drew large crowds. Our football band became quite popular with our lighted uniform caps. We used them as we performed at half time. The stadium lights were turned off and our cap lights added a visual excitement to our performance. Consequently our band was invited to all of the out of town games to play at half time.

In my fifth year at Robinson while at a state contest, a judge who was head of the music department at MacMurray College offered me the position of directing their college choir. This was a great challenge and I accepted his offer. We moved to Jacksonville and joined the MacMurray College staff. This was an enjoyable part of my music career. The choir was very active. We performed at many concert halls spreading the name and quality of this dynamic school. We were quite thrilled to give a concert at Chicago's Orchestra Hall. While at MacMurray College, I became involved in judging high school band contests and I organized a state wide

500 piece band festival and a 250 voice choral festival. Conducting these large groups of talented high school students was indescribable.

In my spare time I directed the Jacksonville Methodist Church Choir, helped the Illinois College for Men form a choral group and directed the local chapter of the Society for the Preservation of Barbershop Quartets whose harmony I truly enjoy to this day.

During that year, I met a band director who had started a soft ice cream store in Springfield Illinois and it had provided him with a nice summer income. That sounded like a good idea, so I found a good location in Virden Illinois (twenty miles from Jacksonville), bought a soft ice cream machine and was in business by the end of the school year. Two weeks later I added a root beer machine and more than doubled my income. I was really enjoying that business when I received a phone call from the superintendent of schools in Champaign Illinois. He told me that the high school vocal position was going to be open and he offered me the job. Years before I had applied for that position thinking it was the number one high school job in the state. I accepted this opportunit, sold my Virden venture and made plans to move to Champaign, Illinois.

Jim Griggs, who directed the Champaign High School Orchestra, was a great help to us. He found us a place to rent, introduced us to the area and helped us move. Once again the quality of the students there was exceptional, just like at Robinson. They accepted me and my leadership. At our first chorus rehearsal, as soon as I heard the tone quality of our two leading sopranos, and the range and quality of two top tenors, I knew I could develop a fine group.

The University of Illinois offered many opportunities for private lessons. I was able to get about 30 % of my choir members to take advantage of this opportunity. I spent a lot of time with our small groups, the boys' troubadours, the madrigal singers (a 16 voice mixed group) and the Modernaires, (a quintet that sang close harmony popular music). These groups became very popular and were in constant demand. They were the main core of my concert choir. This was the finest choir of my career. I remember a judge at the state contest just after we had sung Randell Thompson's Alleluia, commented, "A super choir – I would not have believed it if I hadn't heard it." I continued the musical moods programs that we presented in Robinson. They again were highly successful and drew capacity crowds.

Directing church choirs was and still is a priority of my musical endeavors. While in Champaign, I was asked to direct the Methodist Church Youth Choir ages 14 to 20. I enhanced it with 4 college singers (the best soprano, alto, tenor and base in the university choir.) I paid them with the salary that the church offered me. This was money well spent. You would not believe what those four singers did for that choir. There were 50 singers in the choir and we sang an anthem in the first service every Sunday. I continued directing this choir for our 25 years in Champaign.

My three years assignment at Champaign High School was a delightful experience. This ended my teaching career. In 1953 the Dog n Suds venture started and another adventure began.

ROBINSON HIGH SCHOOL
MUSIC DEPARTMENT

DON'S CHAMPIONSHIP BAND - ROBINSON, IL. HIGH SCHOOL - 1950

DON'S SWEEPSTAKES WINNING CHOIR

A GREAT EXPERENCE

AFTER SEVERAL MONTHS OF PERSUASION, WE WERE TALKED INTO FORMING A HIGH SCHOOL
DANCE BAND AND LOOKING FOR A SUMMER JOB. WE ENDED UP WITH A 10 WEEK CONTRACT
AT INDIANA BEACH RESORT. THE KIDS EARNED $40.00 & WE EARNED $100.00 PER WEEK.
I USED – WE – BECAUSE MARGERET WAS ACTIVE AND NEEDED AS THE BAND MOTHER.
THAT WAS GREAT MONEY FOR THOSE DAYS. THAT INCLUDED A BUNK HOUSE FOR THE KIDS &
A COTTAGE FOR US. AFTER 3 WEEKS OF HARD PLAYING, OUR 1st TRUMPETER'S LIP STARTED
SLIPPING ON THE HIGH NOTES - SO - WE HIRED A PROFESSIONAL 1st TRUMPET – MOVED
OUR 1st TO 2nd – OUR 2nd to 3RD AND HE SPLIT THE TIME WITH OUR 3rd TRUMPETER SO WE
DIDN'T HAVE TO SEND HIM HOME. THE RESORT OWNER SUGGESTED THAT WE SET UP A STAND
NEXT TO THE DANCE HALL – LIKE AT A CARNIVAL – WHERE YOU COULD SHOOT GUNS USING
NICKELS AS BULLETS – AND ATTEMPT TO KNOCK ITEMS OFF OF A SHELF–FOR A PRIZE. WE
SET UP THE STAND – BOUGHT THE GUNS =– AND L,ET THE TWO 3rd TRUMPETERS SHARE TIME
OPERATING THE STAND & PLAYING 3rd TRUMPET. IT WORKED OUT WELL FINANCIALLY' AND WE
DIDN'T HAVE TO SEND ANYONE HOME. THE BAND SOUNDED FINE – BOB BURGESS, OUR 1st
TROMBONIST, DEVELOPED INTO MARVELOUS MUSICIAN – IN FACT HE LATER JOINED THE
STAN KENTON BAND – WHICH WAS THE NUMBER ONE BIG BAND IN THE COUNTRY AT THAT TIME.
HE GAVE THE BAND A LOT OF CLASS WITH HIS TERRIFIC SOLOS. – *as ca. Ha..w..k...*

WE PLAYED 10 WEEKS AT INDIANA BEACH
ON LAKE SHAFFER

OUR HIGH SCHOOL DANCE BAND

Robinson Musicians Win State Crown

ROBINSON HIGH SCHOOL MUSIC DEPARTMRENT WINS
STATE SWEEPSTAKES AWARD FOR SECOND STRAIGHT YEAR.

Scores 104 Points Out Of Possible 108

High School Music-
ians Carry Off High
Honors In State Meet
On Saturday.

Local Musicians Win Top Honors In State Finals

Robinson High School
Music Department
Repeats High Honor
For Second Straight
Year.

Robinson chalked up a total of 143 points out of a possible 150 points. Last year Robinson won the sweepstakes by scoring 104 points out of a possible 108.

The Robinson High School student body paid homage to Director Don Hamacher and his prize winning musicians with a special assembly at the school this morning when the winning trophies were presented to the

A GREAT BUNCH OF TALENTED STUDENTS
AND A LOT OF HARD WORK PAID BIG DIVIDENDS

MUSICAL MOODS

DURING MY FIRST YEAR AT ROBINSON HIGH SCHOOL, I DESIGNED AND
PRESENTED A PROGRAM THAT WE NAMED MUSICAL MOODS.
IT WAS A 3 MOOD PROGRAM WITH COSTUMES AND SCENERY. THE FIRST
MOOD WAS ALWAYS RELIGIOUS -- THE SECOND MOOD CHANGED EVERY
YEAR -- GAY 90's -- COLLEGE SERENADE -- GOLDEN OLDIES -- ETC. THE
THIRD MOOD WAS ALWAYS POPULAR BIG BAND MUSIC. THE PROGRAM
WAS A BIG SUCCESS SO WE PRESENTED IT EVERY YEAR.

CHS Musicians' Versatility Shown In 'Musical Moods'

By BILL ALLEN
News-Gazette Staff Writer

Versatile, appealing both to the
eye and ear, and completely entertaining was the Champaign
High School music department's
second production of "Musical
Moods" staged Friday night in
the Champaign Junior High
School gymnasium.

Even though the religious and
college moods were well done, the
final modern mood brought the
most applause from the audience
and displayed the finest caliber

There were no stars of the show
as billed, but if there had been
a star, it would be personable
Larry Hill who sang in the a ca-
pella choir for the first mood, directed the boy's chorus in the
second mood, and sparkled as a
dance band soloist in the final
mood.

But Hill was not alone in his
triple role Friday night. Dozens
of other students participated in
all three moods as vocalists, in-
strumentalists, or dancers.

RELIGIOUS MOOD

MUSICAL MOODS
1945 thru 1950

GAY 90's MOOD

Musical Moods Packs Gym Here For Performance

Plan Greatest Musical Moods In Past Years

Music Lovers Give
...gh Praise To Local
Musical Presentation
Last Night.

Nearly 3,000 music lovers of
Robinson and Crawford county
packed the Robinson High

Production Will
Feature Religious,
Romantic and Modern
Periods.

150 students of music department of Robinson High School
have been working like trojans
for the past several weeks putting on the finishing touches to

POPULAR MOOD

25

The
ILLINOIS

MUSIC EDUCATOR

NOVEMBER-DECEMBER, 1949

Illinois Chorus PUBLISHED IN THE
INTEREST OF CHORAL
MUSIC IN ILLINOIS

Vol. II   ROBERT P. COMMANDAY, Editor   No. 2

ROBINSON
HIGH SCHOOL OF THE MONTH

Robinson's Choral groups, ensembles, and soloists brought home the 1949 Class B Sweepstakes Trophy, piling up points with the mixed choir, boys' and girls' glee clubs, vocal and instrumental organization. Leaving at home his 65 piece band, well-known in Southeastern Illinois for its precise playing and imaginative drills, Hamacher placed Division I in almost all other sections of the State finals.

Three choral organizations, 16 ensembles, and 9 soloists participated, with frequently two or more groups or soloists competing in one category. The top honors that Robinson carried off were a tribute to the fine training and enthusiasm with which his students approached the contest.

Music Program Varied and Full

The Robinson Music Department, a one-man operation, is not as might be inferred, merely a contest-producer, but presents an active educational program. By the time Christmas rolls around this year, Robinson will have participated in three major fall choral clinics and festivals: Eastern Illinois State College, "EI" Festival (as hosts), All-State High School Activity. They will have presented their band concert (November 17), their annual Christmas concert, and will have been well into preparations for a band clinic and the big February concert, "Musical Moods."

The February show presents three musical moods, Religious, Romantic and Modern, with scenery, costumes and artwork prepared by a student committee for each "mood". The glee clubs, choir, solos and duets supply variety and contrast in the Romantic Mood, while unusual ensemble groups, both vocal and instrumental, keep up a fast pace in the Modern Mood.

How much of the students' educational needs are supplied by this predominantly applied program (Hamacher also teaches a General Music Class)? Suffice it to say that Robinson's music-makers demonstrate a happy and healthy respect for music and the enjoyment that they derive from it; that in winning the Sweepstakes, all the groups showed a sight-singing ability and a music vitality which evoked unanimously enthusiastic judges' comments. Our congratulations to Don Hamacher and to Superintendent-Principal Olson, whose support has developed an outstanding program at Robinson.

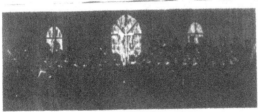

Robinson High School Choir

Don Hamacher

THE HAMACHERS MOVE TO JACKSONVILLE
MAC MURRAY COLLEGE FOR GIRLS
JACKSONVILLE, ILL. 1950 - 51

MAC MURRAY COLLEGE WAS AN ALL GIRLS SCHOOL IN 1950. AT THAT TIME
IT HAD AN ENROLLMENT OF 950 STUDENTS.
JOE CLEELAND, THE HEAD OF THEIR MUSIC DEPT. HAD JUDGED MY CHOIRS
AT THE STATE CONTEST AND OFFERED ME THE POSITION IN THEIR MUSIC DEPT.
I REMEMBER HE HAD WRITTEN ON THE JUDGES COMMENT SHEET.
(A PROFESSIONAL JOB - I WOULD NOT HAVE BELIEVED IT IF I HADN'T HEARD IT)
I WOULD BE DIRECTING THEIR CHOIR & BAND -- AMONG OTHER THINGS.
THE CHOIR MET EVERYDAY & THE BAND MET 3 TIMES EACH WEEK.
THE CHOIR PERFORMED AT THE COLLEGE VESPER SERVICE EVERY WED.
THE BAND GAVE ONE CONCERT PER YEAR AND THE DANCE BAND PLAYED FOR
MANY OCCASIONS. THE CHOIR SANG AT VARIOUS CHURCHES, ORGANIZATIONS, RADIO
STATIONS, ETC. ---ADVERTISING THE COLLEGE --- OUR MOST EXCITING PERFORMANCE WAS
AT ORCHESTRA HALL IN CHICAGO. THE COLLEGE OWNED A BUS AND THEY SENT OUR
35 SINGER CHOIR ALL THROUGH THE STATE -- DOING ABOUT 20 OF THOSE MISSIONS
DURING THE YEAR. TWO OTHER JOBS WERE INCLUDED WITH THIS JOB TO MAKE UP MY
TOTAL SALARY. -- DIRECTING THE JACKSONVILLE METHODIST CHURCH CHOIR & DIRECTING
THE S. P. E. B. S. Q. S. A. BARBERSHOP CHORUS.
ALL IN ALL, IT WAS AN ENJOYABLE YEAR -- AND I BELIEVE THAT IT HELPED ME LAND
---- WHAT I THOUGHT WAS THE BEST HIGH SCHOOL JOB IN THE STATE -- CHAMPAIGN, ILL...

Main Hall

Music Hall

JOE CLEELAND
HEAD OF
MUSIC DEPARTMENT

COLLEGE CHAPEL

Grace Methodist Church

MAC MURRAY COLLEGE

CHOIR

BAND

MADRICALS

METHODIST CHURCH CHOIR

THE MAC MURRAY CHOIR LOVED TO TRAVEL

READY TO LEAVE FOR CHICAGO

OUR PERFORMANCE HERE IN ORCHESTRA
HALL WAS QUITE EXCITING!! 1951

DIRECTING MASS ORGANIZATIONS & JUDGING
SHOWS AND CONTESTS WERE ALWAYS EXCITING

RHS Music Director, Don Hamacher,
Serves As Judge For College Show

Mr. Don Hamacher

Name Hamacher One Of Judges Of Student Revue

In recognition for his outstanding work in the production of "Musical Moods" for the past six years at the Robinson High School, Don Hamacher, director of music of the local school, has been selected as one of the judges for the 17th annual campus revue at the Indiana State Teachers College at Terre Haute.

DIRECTED SEVERAL GROUPS IN JACKSONVILLE

JACKSONVILLE BARBERSHOP CHORUS

ILLINOIS COLLEGE CHOIR
BOYS LOVED TO SING

SEVENTEEN BANDS IN A FESTIVAL

31

THE HAMACHERS MOVE TO CHAMPAIGN IN 1951

CHAMPAIGN METHODIST CHURCH T

MY YOUTH CHOIR SANG EVERY SUNDAY

AFTER RENTING FOR A YEAR, WE BUILT THIS TRI--LEVEL
HOME AND LIVED THERE UNTIL WE MOVED IN 1975 TO
NORTH MYRTLE BEACH.

CHAMPAIGN HIGH SCHOOL CHOIR

THIS WAS A FINE CHOIR - THE BEST THAT I HAD EVER
DIRECTED. THEY BLENDED WELL AND THEY TOOK ON THE
TONE QUALITY OF OUR TWO BEST SOPRANOS. THEIR
ATTITUDES WERE GREAT AND THEY ENJOYED SINGING,

I WAS ESPECIALLY PLEASED AT THE JUDGES COMMENTS
WHERE THEY NOTICED THE HIGH CALIBER OF MUSIC THAT
WE CHOSE TO SING. RANDELL THOMPSON'S (ALLELUIA) &
HINDEMITH'S (SINCE ALL IS PASSING).

CHAMPAIGN HIGH SCHOOL ENSWMBLES

TROUBADORS
THEY WERE THE MALE PART OF OUR CHOIR
THEY WERE A FUN GROUP AND POPULAR WITH THE PUBLIC.

MADRIGALS

THIS GROUP CONSISTED OF MY VERY BEST SINGERS.
THEYDRESSED FORMALLY AND SANG INTERESTING SONGS.
THEY QUICKLEY BECAME OUR MOST POPULAR GROUP;.

MOODS - A BIG HIT IN CHAMP[AIGN

WE REPEATED OUR MUSICAL MOODS TYPE PROGRAMS
HERE IN CHAMP[AIGN

THE BIG BAND BAND SOUND WITH THE MODERNAIRES

MODERNAIRES

ch 8 B

TRIPS WE TOOK DURING OUR 25 YRS. IN CHAMPAIGN AND BEFORE.

1948 - LAKE HURON, CANADA - CAMPING WITH HERB & MARILYN NORTON
1949 - DROVE TO MIAMI WITH JIM & ERMA BIEHL TO A KIWANIS CONVENTION
1950 - DROVE TO N. Y. CITY WITH JIM & MARGARET GRIGGS TO A MUSIC CONV
1952 - NEW YORK CITY WITH JIM & MARGARET GRIGGS TO A MUSIC CONVENTION
1953 - FLEW TO MIDLAND, MICH. IN RENTED TRI-PACER WITH INSTRUCTOR
1954 - FLEW TO MACKINAW ISLAND WITH LLOYD & DORIS WORDEN IN HIS PLANE
1955 - ELEW TO BROADMOOR HOTEL IN COLO. SPRINGS WITH THE WORDENS
1956 - FLEW NORM & JEAN PATTON TO NORTHERN AIR RESORT, WISC.-TRIPACER
1957 - FLEW TO SHAWNEE ON THE DELEWARE WITH THE WORDENS
1958 - FLEW ABE SAPPERSTEIN-HARLEM GLOBE TROTTER'S COACH TO CHICAGO
1959 - FLEW OUR GIRLS TO WEST END ISLAND IN OUR TRIPACER
1960 - FLEW OUR TRIPACER TO THE KY. DERBY FOR OUR FIRST TIME
1961 - SPENT A WEEK ON KY LAKE - OUR FAMILY WITH THE SMITHS & NUNNILEES
1962 - FLEW TO BROADMOOR HOTEL AS THEIR GUESTS - CONVENTION SITE HUNTING
1963 - FLEW TO DEAUVILLE HOTEL-FLA.-AS THEIR GUESTS-CONVENTION SITE HUNTING
1964 - JAN. - WE FLEW OUR GIRLS TO THE ROSE BOWL AND MET THE SMITHS
1964 - MAR. DOG N SUDS CONVENTION -DEAUVILLE HOTEL - MIAMI, FLA.
1964 - WE TOOK OUR GIRLS FOR A TWO WEEK TOUR OF EUROPE
1965 - FLEW TO HOLLYWOOD BCH. HOTEL FLA. AS GUESTS - CONVENTION SITE HUNTING
1965 - MAR. - WE FLEW GLORIA & HOWARD TO FLA. IN OUR NEW TWIN COMANCHEE
1965 - JUNE - A REUNION IN INDIANAPOLIS WITH THE HOODS & BIEHLS & THEIR GIRLS
1965 - DEC. - WE FLEW OUR GIRLS TO THE BAMAHAS IN OUR NEW TWIN COMANCHEE
1966 - FEB. - SPENT A WEEK IN JAMAICA WITH THE GOURMET GROUP
1966 - JUNE - SPENT A WEEK IN CALLOWAY GARDENS GA. GOLFING WITH THE CROSBYS

1966 - JULY - 3-M PEOPLE FLEW ME TO 1000 LAKES CANADA - WEEK ON THEIR BOAT
1966 - NOV - WE FLEW BOB SMITH TO MEXICO CITY & MET CHRIS THERE FOR A WEEK
1967 - JAN. - WE FLEW TO WINTER PARK, COLO. FOR A WEEK OF SKI-ING
1967- MAR. - WE FLEW LOU & EMILY BURTIS TO FREEPORT ISLAND FOR WEEK
1967- JUN. - WE FLEW HOWIE & CONNIE MARTIN TO THE EXPO. IN MONTREAL CANADA
1968- FEB - WE WENT SKI-ING IN ASPIN, COLO, WITH CHAMPAIGN GROUP
1968 - MAY - WE SPENT A WEEK AT KY. LAKE WITH THE SMITH FAMILY
1968- MAR- WE WENT TO PORTUGAL & SPAIN WITH A CHAMPAIGN GROUP
1968- JUN. - WE FLEW INTO A SMALL GRASS STRIP TO VISIT THE GILLS-- SOUTHERN, ILL
1968- DEC.- WE FLEW OUR GIRLS & HUSBANDS TO FLA - 6 IN OUR PLANE
1969- JAN - WE FLEW TO ELUTHERA ISLAND FOR OUR 25th WEDDING ANIVERSARY
1969 - FEB. - WE FLEW ALONE TO KEY WEST & VISITED THE AUSTINS ON THE WAY
1970 - FEB - WE ATTENDED OUR DOG N SUDS CONVENTION IN LAS VEGAS
1970 - DEC. - WE FLEW OUR GIRLS & HUSBANDS AGAIN TO FLA. WE STAYED A MONTH
1971 - JUNE - WE CRUISED THE MEDITERRANEAN SEA--ATHENS TO EPHESOS WITH ILLINI
1972 - MAR - WE WENT ON A DOG N SUDS POST CONVENTION CRUISE TO CURACAO
1972 - JUNE - WE FLEW TO LAKE GENEVA, WISC--A WEEK WITH OUR GOURMET GROUP
1973 - MAR - WE WENT ON A DOG N SUDS POST CONVENTION TRIP TO MOROCO, AFRICA
1974 - MAR - WE WENT ON A DOG NSUDS POST CONVENTION TRIP TO MEXICO CITY

CHAPTER FIVE:
Always the Entrepreneur

The title, "Always the Entrepreneur" describes Don Hamacher very well.

At the age of fourteen he helped his father who owned a flour mill. Don's job was to take orders for flour, cornmeal and salt from the local grocery stores and then help the truck driver with the deliveries. At sixteen, Don organized a dance band and played weekends locally and in nearby towns. The summer after his senior year in high school, he booked his band for the summer at Lake Maur Resort in Excelsior Springs, Missouri. That was back in the days when they had a fence around the dance floor and you paid five cents to get on the dance floor and dance to a medley of three tunes. While at Missouri University he started a dance band booking agency; and booked his band and the other two local bands for sorority and fraternity dances. This business was quite profitable. That summer, Don and his room mate, Lloyd Story went to Chicago to look for a dance band job. When they got there, they found that they needed a union card to play and it took six weeks to sweat out a card. So they started looking for other employment. Their first job was in a meat packing company. They packed bacon in cans for the army. They stayed there about a week. Next they found a better paying job-making shells. This job required them to be able to read a micrometer. They solved this problem by calling a machine shop and asking if there was someone there who could teach them to read a micrometer. Lloyd and Don were invited to visit the shop and in one hour mastered the task. The next day they started the new job.

During the war it was easy to find work. After a week there, they spotted an ad in the newspaper about building the Chrysler building and the need for hod carriers. The job paid big money—$1.25 an hour with lots of time-and-a-half and double-time. They jumped on that job quickly. This new challenge turned out to be a shoveing, dirt-digging job. Don will never forget the first day during a chat with his straw boss. When Don told him he was senior in college, the boss couldn't believe that he was digging dirt with men who could hardly speak English. Right then he took Don to the big boss who offered him a much better job. The new "work" assignment was checking equipment and their operators. At the beginning of each shift, using a golf cart, Don drove around and checked that all operators were present and operating their equipment. He repeated that chore toward the end of the shift which took about two-and-a half hours for each run so he had about three hours free in the middle of the shift. The boss told Don that he could go any place or do anything as long as he got the checking done. Don did all kinds of things during that time. He slept, read, shopped at nearby stores and brought food and drinks to the operators who considered him their errand boy. Occasionally Don went to the movies during his generous break time.

Don purchased a car for $35.00 and made $5.00 per day hauling workers to and from the train station to add to the growing cash reserve. It was a fun and profitable summer. Don would go downtown with Lloyd in the evenings to the hotels and listen to the big bands. They could buy a drink at the bar in the back of the ballroom and listen without paying a cover charge. They knew how to get the most for their hard-earned dollars.

Editor's note: This description of the summer of 1942 seemed to exemplify what an ambitious, innovative businessman Don Hamacher always was by nature.When he recognized an opportunity, he took it. No wonder he experienced so much success and satisfaction throughout his life.

CHAPTER SIX:
The Dog N Suds Story

What do two Champaign, Illinois schoolteachers do to make money during the summer of 1953? Anything they can, of course, but in Don Hamacher and Jim Griggs' case they set up a drive-in root beer and hot dog stand which eventually expanded into a franchise operating in thirty-eight states and Canada. The journey of this small, comfortable business to its final destination is filled with interesting, kind, smart, and daring people. Add to that the built-in Midwest work ethic and fun-loving attitude, then any project has to succeed.

During the school year Jim Griggs led the high school orchestra and Don conducted the concert choir and and vocal groups. Obviously, these partners were not interested in giving up their music careers but forged ahead together developing the summertime project. Jim was acquainted with a graduate student in the nearby university school of architecture and talked him into designing a building that turned out to be a butterfly-winged structure. That original design prevailed as the company expanded. The name Dog N Suds appeared on the student's sketches (he referred to root beer as suds) and the name stuck. This budding architect went on to become part of the Frank Lloyd Wright firm.

The fledgling partners had hoped to bring in $100.00 a day but actually the receipts from day one consistently reached $300.00. Their first Dog N Suds was opened just one week when a woman stopped in and posed lots of questions about the business. She asked if this was a franchise, claiming that she was interested in opening one herself. The new partners, flying by the seat of their business instincts, responded "Why, yes". When she asked, "How old is the franchise?" They confessed, "Lady, it was only conceived when you asked the question." Fortunately, this woman had a sense of humor and the partners helped her set up a business in nearby Rantoul, Illinois. They became fast friends and she did wonders in spreading the good word about Dog N Suds.

Growing from a single drive-in establishment to a countrywide franchise was not a simple two-man project. Enter the attorney, John Franklin, who helped in finding the first location, copyrighting the name, financing the project, and giving general legal advice. Don recalled that John constantly laughed and confessed that he was "watching you boys". Jim Griggs also gave violin lessons to John Franklin's children, a sacrifice which helped solidify the business connection and a strong friendship.

A recent email from Donna Matteson, a former member of Don's high school choir in 1954 who became the secretary of the budding business, gives a clear picture of how and why Dog N Suds succeeded. She wrote: *You have had many accomplishments but the two that stand out in my mind were your ability as a music director and your risky venture into the Dog N Suds root beer franchise. With regard to your musical career, under your direction at our local high school, our music program was continuously rated excellent in all competitive categories from the choir to the Madrigals to the Modernaire group. One event that we all* remember as students was Musical Moods…a fantastic production that was never equaled. Then in 1954 you and another fellow musician, James Griggs, took a chance and hired me as your secretary. What an adventure that was. We were able to experience building a business from the ground up. You and Jim were excited about the possibility of being able to provide a reasonable investment to teachers to help supplement their summer income. The business started with you marketing Reed and Bell root beer but very soon you developed your own root beer concentrate and equipment. I'll never forget those good old hot dogs and root beer. You and Jim never hesitated to utilize student help to serve as carhops, and today that is one of our fondest memories at our high school reunions when we reflect on our high school days. Your first Dog N Suds operation was on the corner of Prospect and Bradley and was no more than a walk-up stand like you would see at the local fairgrounds. Business boomed and kids and families alike couldn't get enough, so a new store was built just north of the original location. That drive-in pad is still there. Before long there were drive-ins popping up in Champaign-Urbana, and eventually the chain expanded to over 600 drive-ins all over the United States and Canada. None of this success could have happened if you and Jim had not had the vision and had not devoted the time and energy it took to fulfill your dreams, which also helped us to fulfill our own. This glowing testimonial written by Donna Matteson was dated January 20, 2011.

Another student, Don Scott, hired by the Dog N Suds enterprise wrote a very thoughtful letter to Don in 2009. …So, North Myrtle Beach recognizes and appreciates all you've brought to their community. Congratulations! Donna and Phil Matteson sent me a copy of Judy Corley's article describing your being named Grand Marshall of their Christmas Parade. I'll bet you had a ball. And I further bet you 'Sold' the program better than Santa could have…You'd likely be surprised to know how often I've parroted your words 'you may be good, but you have to sell, sell, sell it. You sure sold me on selling it—you made me a believer…I remember *you trusted me to park your brand new car (a Mercury?) when we were running late for a performance at the First Methodist Church. When I stopped to park, another driver ran into me damaging your car. I was hugely upset and scared to have to tell you what happened. You never questioned or blamed me. Thanks for that. Memories of the early days of Dog N Suds are alive and well."*

Don reminisces about the first days of the growing business, *After we started franchising stores, two high school coaches from southern Indiana, Monford Morrow and Wayne Norrick approached us for a franchise. After a few successful years of operation, they requested jobs in the management area. We hired Wayne who became a great salesman and Manfred had the super ability to manage the office and staff responsible for the planning of our important conventions and training school programs. They were an important part of the success of Dog N Suds. We later took them in as minor partners along with an excellent salesman, Dick Blankenship. Of course, Donna Matteson, our first secretary, was a continued inspiration all the way through. We were fortunate to have such a dedicated staff.*

The management staff grew and by 1960, junior partners, directors of public relations, sales, marketing, training school, field operations, shipping, comptroller, bookkeeping, receptionist, executive secretary (Donna Matteson), and many office assistants completed the corporate scene at Dog N Suds. By that time the business had developed its own root beer formula and equipment. A monthly magazine called *Rover* (the mascot) was published to keep all the franchise operators updated on company matters, The marketing people also developed Dog N Suds uniforms, imprinted paper goods, pennants, bumper stickers, toothpick flags, lapel badges, thermos jugs, flashlights and root beer labels. Lots of company conventions in great places: New Orleans, St. Louis, Chicago, Miami, Mexico, Jackson, Mississippi, Las Vegas (of course) gathered the store operators together each year. Post-convention trips were offered to Curacao, Rabat, Africa, Mexico, and Jamaica. The morale was high for good reason. The prestigious Forbes Institution rated the organization at the top among growing franchisers. Ah, the 60's those were the good old days for Dog N Suds.

Don recalls with pride, *That decade was filled with high points for our company. In 1967 I was elected International Franchise Association president and in 1969 became president of the Root Beer Institute.In 1969, Barron's Magazine picked Dog N Suds number one in the industry Thus after twenty-five years of growth, that momentous year proved to be a turning point for the company. John Franklin, the attorney and father-like partner, being in poor health wanted to sell. Jim Griggs was also eager to sell. He had already moved to Central American where he settled down with his third wife who happened to have been the daughter of the Costa Rican presidsnt. We had a buy and sell agreement and they wanted to activate it. This was about the time when many companies were going public and I was interested in taking Dog N Suds public, so I started raising the money to buy their stock. I was able to get four of my friends, Lloyd Worden, Frank Robeson, Tom Harrington and Dick Jones to purchase their stock. I sold them 20% of the company value. Together with my stock, we would own 60%. Next I found the two brokers who had taken McDonalds and Kentucky Fried Chicken public. Ferris Chesley of Horn Blower and Weeks purchased 20%. Bob Seward of Smith Barney purchased the other 20%. At that point, I thought I had the right people to take us public. They both came on my Board of Directors and we worked out a plan to go public. Unfortunately, at that moment, the Minnie Pearl fiasco happened and that killed our chances to go public. There I was with a new board who had totally different ways of running a company. We eventually entered into a sell agreement with American Licensing Company and by 1972 the home office moved to Arlington Heights in the Chicago area. I remained in Champaign. By 1974 Frostie*

Enterprises with headquarters in Camden, New Jersey had purchased all the Dog N Suds stock. With the many changes, Dog N Suds started going downhill rapidly. Our original homespun personalities blended well with our franchisees and we thought of their stores as our own. The different managements that followed used a cold hard business approach and they started losing the franchisees' confidence and support. It might have worked out better if they had not become used to our friendly or rather down-home approach. Many of our stores were ma & pa operations in small towns. Their kids had worked with them in the store. It was a family affair. When the kids left home for college, etc., they sold their corner locations for a big profit. A huge change factor had occurred. Drive-up windows became more popular than carhops. Our original idea had run its course. It was hard to believe that at an earlier growth stage we were headed to go public as a significant company but now had run into a hurdle lacking the right tempered people to lead our company forward.

This bleak picture continued until 1991 when a new chapter in the Dog N Suds story began. Don Van Dame, the son of one of the first franchisees in Lafayette, Indiana and his wife Carol purchased all the rights to Dog N Suds with the intentions of revitalizing the chain with their most loyal franchisees At the same time they started marketing Dog N Suds Root Beer in quart bottles. They sold over a million bottles during that first year billed as "the world's creamiest root beer" The quarts became a hot line in the beverage field.

Countless colorful names and personalities are remembered fondly when Dog N Suds is the focus of thoughts and conversations. John Olson who was the top man in sales had the most outgoing personality and the talent of recalling names without hesitation. He went on to become a senior vice-president of the Radisson Hotel organization. The former marine Hal Madsen was the fellow who brought structure to sales. Fred Rawls was the food expert of the company. because neither Griggs or I knew very much about food preparation, Fred had the necessary knowledge to keep the quality of the products high. The general management had two valuable sidekicks, Glenn Stello and Bill Knack, who kept the day-to-day operations smooth and efficient. Quentin Bowles, and Speedy McDowell were the super employees in charge of shipping. Our company could not have grown without the outstanding field representatives, Don McNutt and Bill Newkirk. Dog N Suds flourished because of these loyal individuals.

Thus the legend of small beginnings to huge outcomes is still being recalled with fondness not only in the Midwest, but also in a beautiful spot in North Myrtle Beach, South Carolina. Many names may have been missed but they know their place and value in the Dog N Suds story.

Editor's note: One particular person must be spotlighted in the Dog N Suds story. Don's faithful wife, Margaret (she likes to be called Maggie because she claims it's much more fun) lived the Dog N Suds adventure on the front line. She developed the original recipe for the Coney Dog sauce that was probably the real reason for the company's success and popularity. Maggie is proof that behind every great root beer president is a creative, refreshing, beautiful woman. A toast to her!

DOG N SUDS - THE VERY BEGINING

Don Hamacher
President

PARTNER

Jim Griggs
Vice President

PARTNER

Donna Matteson
Secretary

AT FIRST WE
SOLD ONLY
CONEY DOGS
& ROOT BEER

WE USED
OUR STUDENTS
FOR CAR HOPS

WE TOOK IN
$300.00 THE
FIRST DAY

POLICE HAD TO
DIRECT TRAFIC
AT NIGHT DURING
THE FIRST WEEK

THE ORIGINAL DOG N SUDS DRIVE-IN

OUR FIRST OFFICE WAS LOCATED IN JIM GRIGGS' BASEMENT. HE LIVED ACROSS THE STREET FROM THE SCHOOL WHERE WE TAUGHT. I REMEMBER GETTING DONNA, A STUDENT IN MY CHOIR, TO HELP US CLEAN OUT THE BASEMENT AND FIX IT INTO AN OFFICE. SHE BECAME OUR SECRETARY AND STAYED WITH US ALL THE WAY. WE STAYED IN THAT OFFICE UNTIL WE MOVED INTO FRANKLIN'S NEW BUILDING.

THE DOG N SUDS CORPORATION WAS FORMED \\\
1954

John Franklin
SECRETARY
PARTNER

Manford Morrow
GENERAL MANAGER
JR. PARTNER

Wayne Norrick
SALES MANAGER
JR. PARTNER

Fred Rawles
Food Consultant

1956 - BUILT A NEW COMPANY OWNED DOG N SUDS DRIVE-IN DOWN THE STREET FROM THE ORIGINAL ONE. WE USED IT FOR OUR TRAINING SCHOOL. WE BROUGHT ON FRED RAWLES, AS OUR FOOD CONSULTANT & HE RAN THE STORE.

1956 - OUR FIRST DOG N SUDS CONVENTION

DOG 'N SUDS
first
CONVENTION
SET SATURDAY
1956

"Dog 'n Suds," once a single
establishment owned by two co-
teachers but now a voluntary
chain of 63 stands, will hold its
first convention from 9:00 a.m.
to p.m. Saturday at the Champaign Moose Club.

Two hundred Dog 'n Suds
Drive-In owners, their families
and managers from Illinois, Indiana, Iowa and Missouri will
attend the convention.

WE HELD OUR 1st DOG N SUDS CONVENTION AT THE CHAMPAIGN
MOOSE CLUB. 200 PEOPLE ATTENDED WHICH REPRESENTED THE
63 STORES THAT WE HAD OPENED BY THAT TIME.
WE HELD AN ANNUAL CONVENTION HERE FOR 6 YRS. THROUGH 1961

1957 - WE STARTED EXPENDING OUR MANAGEMENT STAFF

DICK BLANKENSHIP
CUSTOMER RELATIONS
LATER BECAME A JR. PARTNER
JR. PARTNER

JOHN OLSEN
DIV. SALES MGR.
LATER BECAME A VICE PRES.

DAVE BARRET
MARKETING DIRECTOR

GLEN STELLO
TRAINING SCHOOL DIR
LATER BECAME A VICE PRES

CHARLES TICHENOR
MARKETING DIRECTOR
LATER BECAME A VICE PRES.

HAL MADSEN
FIELD OPERATIONS MGR.
LATER BECAME A VICE PRES.

1960 - BY NOW WE HAVE ADDED MORE STAFF

JIM BARTH
COMPTROLLER

GEORGE PETROV
SHIPPING DEPT. MANAGER

BILL HEERMANS
FIELD REP.

BILL NEWKIRK
FIELD REP.

JERRY RUNYON
FIELD REP.

HARVEY BAILEN
SALES

BILL KNACK
ADV.& PROMOTION

NORM PATTON
FIELD REP.

Donna Matteson
Executive Secretary

Martha Eads
Bookkeeping

Martha MacLean
Secretary

Charlot Cole
Secretary

Mary Jane McGee
Secretary

Nancy Oberto
Receptionist

Sheryl Colbert
Office Assistant

Speedie McDowell
Shipping Department

Pete Bates
Shipping Department

Gary Hansmeier
Shipping Department

51

1960 - WE BUILT OUR NEW OFFICE BUILDING

Dog n' Suds Home Office

Here is where the Dog n' Suds Home Office staff works. This new, modern building was completed in July, accommodating a staff of 22.

Let's look at the proud staff on the job in their new quarters:

Champaign, Illinois

Mrs. Nancy Oberto, Receptionist, and Visitor

Left to Right, Front to Back: Mrs. Mary Jane McGee, Mrs. Martha MacLean, Mrs. Charlot Cole, Miss Gladys Mayer, Mrs. Nancy Oberto and Miss Sheryl Colbert in the General Office Room.

Dave Barrett, Director of Customer Relations and a training group in the Conference Room

Left to Right: Mrs. Bernice Jensen, Mr. Jim Barth, Head Bookkeeper, Mrs. Martha Eads, and Miss Gladys Mayer.

1961 - DOG N SUDS FIRST TRAINING FACILITY

Training Program

All new Dog n' Suds operators are trained in all aspects of drive-in operation. Training is given at the Dog n' Suds Office Building and at Fred Rawles' Dog n' Suds on Prospect Avenue in Champaign, Ill.

Topics covered are: Preparing for the Opening, Operations, Menu Planning, Cost Control, Merchandising and Promotion, Selection and Training of Personnel, Bookkeeping.

Fred's Dog n' Suds is operated by Fred Rawles, a well-known food specialist, and his experienced staff. All trainees spend several days with Fred, witnessing his operation first hand and receiving valuable on-the-job training and experience. Here are some shots of Fred's Drive-In, with his competent staff in action:

Fred's Dog n' Suds

FRED'S DOG N' SUDS IN ACTION

Left to right: Barbara Sommer, Jim Ebbing, Assistant to Fred; Judy Richardson, Ronnie Simmons, Fred Rawles, Judy Johnson, Dorothy Ball.

Barbara Sommer, preparing a shake.

Left to right: Barbara Sommer, Jim Ebbing and Jim Myer

1961 - STARTED PUBLISHING OUR MONTHLY MAGAZINE FOR OUR OPERATORS UNDER OUR MASCOT'S NAME
ROVER

ROVER

PUBLISHED BY DOG n SUDS, INC. / CHAMPAIGN, ILL.

DOG n SUDS DRIVE-INS Coast to Coast

PRODUCTS BEING MARKETED

IMPRINTED PAPER

Everything You Need To

PROMOTE FOR PROFIT

Dog n Suds Uniforms

MANAGEMENT TRAINING PROGRAMS

BY 1962 - OUR MONTHLY MANAGEMENT TRAINING SCHOOL
HAD GROWN AND WAS ATTENDEND BY AROUND 20 NEW
OPERATORS EACH SESSION.

1962 - WE STARTED A SERVICE REPRESENTATIVE PROGRAM.
WE SELECTED 20 OF OUR BEST OPERATORS TO ASSIST US
WITH THE OPENING OF NEW STORES.

DOG N SUDS
PLAN BIG CANADIAN EXPANSION

Charles LaPoint, Canadian sales manager for Dog n Suds Ltd., uses a large wall map to point out the province of Saskatchewan, where the Canadian sales office is located. Enjoying this lesson in geography are Dave Yip, seated to LaPoint's right, president of the Canadian organization; Peter Golf, Canadian Dog n Suds pioneer and a veteran drive-in operator in the far north; and Jim Griggs, vice president of Dog n Suds, Inc. Standing is Cecil Lubeck, who will be the business manager for the new Canadian development firm.

1963 - DOG N SUDS 8th CONVENTION
PICK CONGRESS HOTEL IN CHICAGO

500 PEOPLE REPRESENTING 300 STORES
ATTENDED THIS, OUR 8th CONVENTION

DEAUVILLE HOTEL - MIAMI BEACH
PERFECT SITE FOR THE DOG N SUDS 1965 CONVENTION

NEARLY 700 PEOPLE, REPRESENTING 450 STORES ATTENDED
THIS CONVENTION IN MIAMI BEACH.

OUR TABLE WITH MY FAMILY AND ENTERTAINER WOO WOO STEVENS
ROE BARTLE, CHIEF BOY SCOUT EXECUTIVE , WAS OUR SPEAKER

DOG N DUDS CONVENTIONS
AND POST CONVENTION TRIPS

DOG N SUDS CONVENTIONS
AND POST CONVENTION TRIPS

1966 - DOG N SUDS STARTED NAT'L ADVERTISING

DON APPEARED ON THE - TO TELL THE TRUTH PROGRAM

NAT'L, T V SHOW WITH RALPH COLLIER

CHAPTER SEVEN:
Big Sister Speaks

The beauty and wonder of this special segment exists in the fact that one of Don's older sisters, Mary Agnes has taken the time to offer important input into the retelling of her younger brother's life story. At this writing she is ninety-five years young and Don the Younger is a mere ninety. He evidently informed his siblings of the fact that he was having his worldly experiences documented for the purpose of sharing them with the world and with anyone who may profit from reading about his "dolce vita". His sister Mary's written response and her enlightening ideas are not only priceless and concise but also perfectly handwritten without a single spelling error. In this world of glaring grammatical errors and daily mistakes in many publications, the meticulous expression of her thoughts is impressive. She uses many exclamation marks and stars to emphasize the importance of her points and underlines many names and important places to drive home an important point.

In Mary's introduction she advises Don to stress the following important points and people: She writes, 1. *Your inheritance from a musical family—your mother was a talented singer, pianist, painter and poet. Your father as well was an accomplished mandolinist and singer. Both were college graduates in 1909 and 1911 which was rare indeed. 2. Don, you inherited Father's business acuity. Ray Countians called him "a mathematical wizard" 3. The financial and legal support of John Franklin, the attorney, believed in your Dog N Suds dream. 4. Your partner Jim Griggs made possible the architectural drawing of the first new store which became the symbol of your stores forever. 5. A very talented efficient secretary Donna kept you on your toes financially and socially. 6. Your wife, Margaret, your life partner supported and believed in all your financial, social and educational endeavors! Don, I hope all these thoughts will help you with your book. I will want a copy. Love from your sister, Mary*

The heart of Mary's four page carefully crafted letter included the following revealing tribute to her brother for his role in improving her family's situation early in life: : *"Joining the Dog N Suds chain in 1955 made a decisive difference in my family's life style—from struggling farmers to fast food operators! We, my husband E.L. and I, didn't grow up on farms but as young parents were managing E.L.'s mother's small farm of 160 acres and sharing the profits—if any! When the years 1951 to 1955 were declared the driest ever in western Missouri, our Kansas City area was declared a disaster area. Farmers' crops of wheat and corn brought no profit. Livestock raising was a failure. Banks were doing their best to help out with loans to distressed farmers. In the meantime Brother Don, a high school music teacher, had been in Champaign, Illinois since 1951. His reports of his teaching successes, the exciting environment of the area, the great university were positive and exciting. Our 'tales of woe" of crop failure and financial trouble were scary and disheartening. We thought, "How do we as parents of two intelligent young sons educate them beyond their high school years?*

Enter Don's business adventure Dog N Suds. Many young teachers in the summer were moonlighting to supplement their salaries. In three consecutive summers the venture snowballed. Yes, it was so successful that Don called Mary and E.L. to come over to Champaign-Urbana t help him for the summer and maybe the extended season."

Mary reports, *We came, loved it, and managed the first Dog N Suds for years to come. Yes, we left (here a smiley face was drawn with a frown) our beloved Richmond, Missouri, our close friends and family (fourteen first cousins), and a friendly town, small enough to know everybody and their grandparents. Our roots were there and we were close enough to Kansas City to partake in educational advantages."*

"Were we sorry? No. It was a whirlwind of excitement as truly successful Dog N Suds managers in a small college town. Yet it was a shock to twelve year old Brad and fifteen year old Richard to leave their beloved friends, their grandparents and cousins, the rolling hills and woods of Missouri, a hunter and fisherman paradise and move to Champaign, Illinois to a county with all flat lands with nary a rise in the road."

"Eventually Dog N Suds changed all this for the better. All the fifteen to nineteen year olds particularly from brother Don's students vied for employment as carhops at Dog N Suds. We had a payroll of nineteen t twenty kids a day—all wonderful kids—the cream of the crop. Thus our boys got acquainted with a host of new friends. That did it and our bank account grew."

Editor's note Mary further explained that she went on to teach school in nearby Rantoul for four years, then spent the rest of her career in Champaign. She earned a BA and Masters of Music in piano. She was a church organist and to this day still plays for special occasions that you will learn more about shortly. Mary joined many social and civic clubs and became well known as a performing pianist, piano teacher and accompanist. Mary writes that she loved the musical cultural advantages afforded by the university, hearing five star artists and well-known orchestras much the same as in Chicago.

"My husband took another job as a field manager for the Henry Gill Co., a truck and track equipment firm. "We were financially secure and educated our sons through their bachelor degrees. We had reached our goal. Emotionally and socially E.L. always missed our little hometown of Richmond, Missouri probably more than I did. He died of a massive heart attack on June 21, 1971 having lived with a heart murmur all of his fifty-six years of life."

"So Dog N Suds, my brother's creation, helped to shape our futures in many ways from uncertain farm lives to happy successful lives full of new adventures. At age 95 I miss the obvious family roots but I'm happy with my long life in Champaign. My sons and families are attentive and give me much support and two charming, loving daughters-in-law, four grandchildren (two girls, two boys) and five great grandchildren (four girls and one boy). I played the organ at the weddings of two granddaughters, two grandnieces and most recently on December 4, 2010 at my grandson's wedding."

"Thanks to Don and Maggie for our move to Champaign-Urbana in May, 1955 to join the Dog N Suds team".

"P.S. I'll make a photocopy of the Life Story of Lydia Catherine (Lutz) Hamacher—our mother—soon."

Your loving sister,
Mary

BIG SISTER

MARY BATES

64

CHAPTER EIGHT:
Highlights of The Dog N Suds Story

Author's note: The Dog N Suds story would not be complete without the notable thoughts of Don Hamacher. The following thumbnail sketch and chronology came from the Dog N Suds scrapbook which tells the authentic tale through Don's eyes and memory:

- Dog N Suds—The very beginning—1953
- Our first office was located in Jim Griggs' basement. He lived across the street from the school I remember getting Donna, a student in my choir, to help us clean out the basement and fix it into an office.
- At first we sold only Coney dogs and root beer.
- We used our students for car hops.
- We took in $300.00 the first day. Police had to direct traffic at night during the first week.
- The Dog N Suds Corporation was formed in 1954. In 1955 we brought in our first franchise storeowners. Manford Morrow became our General Manager and Wayne Norrick became the Sales Manager. They had been schoolteachers in southern Indiana and eventually became junior partners in our organization.

- In 1956 we built a new Dog N Suds Drive-in down the street from the original. We used it as our training school. We brought in Fred Rawles as our food consultant and he ran the store.
- In 1956 we held our first Dog N Suds convention at the Champaign Moose Club. Two hundred people attended representing sixty-three stores that we had opened by that time. We held an annual convention here for six years through 1961.
- In 1960 we built our new home office building at 702 West Bloomington Road, Champaign, Illinois.
- By 1962 our monthly management training school had grown and was attended by twenty new operators each session.
- Also in 1962 we started a service representatives program. We selected twenty of our best operators to assist in opening new stores.
- Dog N Suds plans big Canadian expansion. The sales office was located in Saskatchewan.
- In 1963 the company's 8th convention was held at Pick Congress Hotel in Chicago with 500 attendees from 300 stores. In 1964 we went back to that hotel with 600 people representing nearly 400 stores.
- In 1965 the convention was in Miami Beach with 700 people from 450 stores. Roe Bartle, the national chief executive of the Boy Scouts of America, was the speaker.
- For the next ten years conventions and convention trips were held at the following: Chase Park Plaza, St. Louis 1967; Arlington Park Hilton, New Orleans, 1968; Chicago, 1969; Jamaica, 1969; Las Vegas, 1970; Curacao, 1971; Rabot, Africa, 1972; Mexico City, 1973; Jackson, Mississippi 1974 and many more good times.
- In 1966 the company started national advertising with my appearance on the popular television program *To Tell the Truth* which Ralph Collier hosted. Don also did a publicity spot for Dog N Suds on another popular TV program *One in a Million* where he accepted the challenge of starting a fire in mere seconds. Don used flint and steel, an old lesson from

his Boy Scout days. Don succeeded in the task and got good publicity for their company at the same time.

- Don was guest speaker at Zeibart Process Corp. annual meeting, then at the 49th National Restaurant-Hotel-Motel Convention in Chicago, he met with forty-two franchising executives at seminar at the Harvard Business School and spoke at the International Franchise Association (IFA) Managers Conference.
- In 1967 he was elected president of the I.F.A. Al Lapin of IHOP was 1st Vice President and Warren Rosenthal of the Long John Silver chain was the treasurer.
- In 1969 he was elected president of the Root Beer Institute.
- That year Dog N Suds was in the Orange Bowl parade in Coral Gables, Florida.
- In 1969 root beer articles appeared in news articles in more than twenty cities, made the front cover of Soft Drink Industry Review magazine, and appeared on the restaurant signs at the exits of interstate highways
- In 1969 Institutions Magazine displayed a page with pictures of present managment perspective. Don's picture was shown with such well known business leaders as Barron Hilton, W. Marriott Jr. and W. Lassidor
- In 1969 many changes took place in the company. Don recalls "With John Franklin retiring and Jim Griggs moving to Central America, many companies were interested in buying us. We decided to activate our buy and sell agreement. They wanted to sell and I wanted to stay so they gave me thirty days to raise the money to buy them out. It only took me one week to come up with the funds. I sold Griggs's and Franklin's stock to four of my local friends and two stock brokers who had taken McDonalds and KFC public. I did this with the hope of taking DognSuds public. Unfortunately the timing was wrong since the Minnie Pearle franchise fiasco took place. They sold franchisees with poor locations just to sell them. Sadly 250 stores went broke in a year. This affected the industry negatively." and ruined the chance to go public.

- In 1970 American Licensing Company, a part of Laird, Inc., a large investment bank and member of the New York Stock Exchange made us an offer and we accepted.
- In 1972 Dog N Suds home office moved to Chicago area. Things were different after the move and the company started losing its personal appeal.
- In 1974 Frostie Enterprises with headquarters in Camden, New Jersey purchased all the Dog N Suds stock. Michael Fessler, then thirty-five years old had inherited the business from his father, Bill, who had been on the Root Beer Institute Board of Directors when Don was president. Michael wanted Don in the company but he declined. Don did accept a consultant position during which he flew to Camden every other week for five years. Don claims that this was a fun job. "Michael and I became good friends. I enjoyed helping him and I got a lot of good flying experience in and out of large eastern cities." A note from Michael to Don in 1990 stated "You taught me well!"
- In 1979 Don retired from his career in business.
- What happened to Dog N Suds? Don's answer: "With the many changes in management, Dog N Suds started going downhill rapidly. Our original home-spun personalities blended well with our franchisees and we thought of their stories as our own. The different managements that followed used a cold, hard business approach and they started losing the franchisee's confidence and support. It might have worked out better if they had not gotten used to our friendly and rather country-style approach. Many of our stores were ma and pa operations in small towns. Their kids had worked for them in the store. It was a family affair. When the kids left home for college, etc. they sold their corner locations for a big profit. A change in times made drive-up windows more popular and convenient than car hops.
- In 1991 a new chapter in the Dog N Suds appeared on the scene. Don Van Dame and Carol, his wife, the son of one of our first franchisees in Lafayette, Indiana, and a partner,

Dick Morath, purchased all the rights of Dog N Suds with the intentions of revitalizing the chain.

- In 1998 the Champaign High School class of 1953 made Dog N Suds the theme of their 45th reunion. Many of these students worked at our original store. Jim Griggs, Don Van Dame, and I attended and were honored to be there. Donna and Phil Matteson were chairpersons of the affair and Quinton Bowles, our high school drummer and Dog N Suds shipping department wonder was also there.

- In 2003 Dog N Suds marketed root beer in bottles. At the October 24th Annual Meeting Don Van Dame stated "A milestone in the sales of Dog N Suds was achieved…in that we were able to generate sales of two million quarts during the past year…Our sales of the 'world's creamiest root beer' in only quart bottles establishes Dog N Suds as one of the hot lines in the beverage field. Also at the request of several supermarket chains, we will have a new twelve ounce brown bottle for our root beer which will be marketed as a four-pack."

Author's note: Hopefully, the itemized approach to the Dog N Suds story provides the most succinct view of the business which remains so much a part of Don and Maggie's vivid memories.

TOP YEARS OF MY BUSINESS CAREER

AMERICAN MANAGEMENT ASSOCIATION

franchises

SEPTEMBER 27-29, 1967 / CHICAGO

Guest Speakers:

GEORGE F. DILLMAN
Vice-President & Secretary
Diversa, Inc.
and
President
Bonanza International, Inc.
Dallas, Tex.

DONALD R. HAMACHER
President
International Franchise
Association
President
Dog n Suds, Inc.
Champaign, Ill.

effective marketing

through

I FELT HONORED TO BE A GUEST SPEAKER
AT THE AMERICAN MANAGEMENT ASSOCIATION

FRANCHISING   *earn a vacation in the sun*

your GOLDEN opportunity

Donald R. Hamacher, president, International Franchise
Assn., kicks off National Franchise Week July 8-16 by
outlining fundamental qualifications and how to get
into this lucrative field as a franchisee including what
this $70 billion industry offers in profit and prestige.

AN ARTICLE IN BARRONS MAGAZINE

TOP YEARS OF MY BUSINESS CAREER

BARRON'S REPORTS DOG N SUDS NUMBER 1.

BARRON'S
August 25, 1969

Hot dogs, which may be more American than apple pie, have specialists too: Lum's, Nathan's Famous, Der Wienerschnitzel and No. 1 in the business, Dog N' Suds, owned by American Licensing Corp. (expected to file a public offering shortly). Roast beef, which had been the province

Continued on Page 18

Barron's magazine, which is a leading national finance and business weekly publication, revealed in the August 25th issue that *Dog n Suds, Inc., is tops* in its field of fast food franchising firms

This is certainly a fine tribute to your company which was originated at Champaign back in 1954 by Don Hamacher and Jim Griggs who were music teachers at the Champaign High School and in the subsequent years has emerged to be one of the leading fast food companies in North America.

INSTITUTIONS MAGAZINE listed Dog n Suds, Inc. as number 76 in the top 400 for recognized companies in the food industry for year ending December 31, 1968. The immediate competitors in our field which were listed by Barron's magazine include Lum's, ranked at 129th. Der Wienersnitzel, ranked at 186th, and Nathan's Famous of New York, ranked at 258th. The INSTITUTION MAGAZINE ranking is considered at the most reliable and authentic to the food industry.

Incidentally, the United States Army is listed as number one in the top 400. This is very notable that your company is ranked and considered as number one in its catagory of fast food franchising industry

The estimated sales of Dog n Suds Drive-In Restaurants during 1968 was $42,000,000. As a franchised dealer of our company, you can certainly be proud and feel a very important part of the food industry in our nation.

TOP YEARS OF MY BUSINESS CARRIER
SPEACHES AND RECOGNITIONS

Don Hamacher
Guest Panelist

Don Hamacher, president of Dog 'n Suds, Inc., 702 W. Bloomington Road, C, will be a guest panelist on the program of the 49th National Restaurant - Hotel - Motel Convention May 20 - 23, in Chicago.

Hamacher will be a member of the panel discussion program on franchise operations.

More than 65,000 delegates are expected to attend the three - day event his year.

NATIONAL RESTAURANT SHOW

Donald R. Hamacher was guest speaker at Ziebart Process Corporation's annual meeting. Roger Waindle, Ziebart President and IFA Director, well understood the value of presenting the Franny award with

'anfare and dignity. Photograph shows **Hamacher** at the inquet, before the entire group, presenting one of six 'ranny's" given that evening. **Roger Waindle** looks on.

SPEAKER AT ZIEBART CONVENTION

INTERNATIONAL FRANCHISING ASSOCIATION

at

HARVARD BUSINESS SCHOOL

certifies that

DON HAMACHER

INVITED TO HARVARD BUSINESS SCHOOL FOR SEMINAR

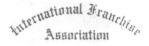

International Franchise Association

presented to

Donald R. Hamacher

in recognition of his participation in and completion of franchise management conference program and for his leadership in advancing the franchise marketing concept.

SPEAKER AT I.F.A. MGR. CONFERENCE

72

TOP YEARS OF MY BUSINESS CAREER

PRESIDENT OF INTERNATIONAL FRANCHISE ASSOCIATION

DON HAMACHER
ELECTED PRESIDENT I.F.A.

1967

Donald R. Hamacher, president of Dog n Suds, Inc. was elected president of the International Franchise Association for 1967. The election took place at a meeting of top franchise executives in Chicago last month.

I.F.A. is an organization made up of 200 of the nation's leading franchisors who work together to promote better franchising. As president of this organization Mr. Hamacher will head association activities for an industry which is called "the fastest growing marketing technique in the nation." Franchise outlets now account for 25% of all retail sales in the United States. Last year, franchising reached $70 billion in gross sales . . . an increase of 23% over 1965.

 NEWSLETTER

INTERNATIONAL FRANCHISE ASSOCIATION
(312) Financial 6-1665
333 North Michigan Avenue • Chicago 60601

OFFICERS

DONALD R. HAMACHER
President . . . . Dog 'n Suds
AL LAPIN, JR.
First VP . . . International Industries, Inc
ROBERT GROVER
Second VP . . . . Snap-on Tools, Inc
WARREN ROSENTHAL
Treasurer . . . . Jerry's Restaurants

DIRECTORS

David Bornow . . Beltone Electronics, Inc
George Brummett . . . . . . Pepsi Cola, Inc
Dansby A. Council . Council Manufacturing
Larry Lehner . . . . . . Mary Carter Paint
Robert Patrick . . White Hen Pantry Division
⠀⠀⠀⠀⠀⠀⠀⠀⠀⠀The Jewel Companies
Monte E. Pendleton . . Sun-X International
Julian Porter . . . . U.S. Mercantile
Sam Preston . . . . Johnson Waxways
Robert Rosenberg . . . . . Dunkin' Donuts
David Slater . . . . Mister Donut
Roger Waindle . . . Ziebart Process Corp

COMMITTEE CHAIRMEN

Education . . . . Robert Rosenberg
Public Relations . . . Monte E. Pendleton
Governmental Relations . . . Al Lapin, Jr
Legal . . . . David Slater
Membership Dev. . . . . George Brummett
International Dev. . . . . . Dansby Council
Ethical Standards . . . . . Robert Grover
Membership Screening . . . . Julian Porter
DSA "Franny" . . . . Larry Lehner
Finance Committee . . . Warren Rosenthal

73

TOP YRS. OF MY BUSINESS CAREER
1969 - PRESIDENT OF ROOT BEER INSTITUTE

Don Hamacher Elected President Root Beer Institute

Left to right: Mr. William T. Reiss of Hires Company, Mr. Richard Coleman Florasynth Laboratories, Inc., Mr. M. A. Cleveland Richardson Corp., Mr. G. E. Kopald Dad's Root Beer Company, Mr. Louis Collins Beverages International, Mr. Don Hamacher Dog n Suds, Inc. Mr. Grant Golden Nedlog Company, Mr. J. Fiorillo Cott Root Beer Company.

OFFICERS
AND DIRECTORS

President
Don Hamacher
Dog n Suds, Inc.

Vice President-Treasurer
Grant Golden
Nedlog Co.

Vice President-Secretary
M. A. Cleveland
RICHardson Corp.

OTHER
DIRECTORS

Richard J. Coleman
Florasynth Laboratories

Louis Collins
The Hires Company
Division of
Beverages International I

Andrew P. Fiorillo
Cott Corporation

William Geib
Ma's Old Fashioned
Bottling, Inc.

Gordon E. Kopald
Dad's Root Beer Co.

Robert H. MacLachlan
J. Hungerford Smith Co., In

E. S. Weber
A & W International, Inc.

CHICAGO DAILY NEWS, Friday, December 26, 1969

Donald Hamacher (left) of Dog 'n' Suds, gets a root beer toast after his election as president of the Root Beer Institute. Congratulations are from Aaron Cushman (center), execut ve director, and G. E. Kopald of Dad's Root Beer Co., past president.

DOG N SUDS REVIVAL

VANDAME'S HEAD DOG N SUDS
DON & CAROL VANDAME

Future Is Great For Dog n Suds

DOG N SUDS MARKETS ROOT BEER IN BOTTLES

Chapter Nine:
Don's Fondest Business Memories

Looking back with pride on one's business career can be rare in today's world. Many executives cannot claim that their experiences were entirely honorable and satisfying. Don Hamacher enjoys endless memories that most assuredly make him smile with contentment. Here he shares some of those times, people and honors.

Flying was my hobby. We flew everywhere both for business and pleasure. I logged over 6,000 hours in the air, starting out with a Piper Tri-pacer, then a 150 HP Comanche, then on to a 250 HP. Comanche, ending up with a new 1966 Twin Comanche. I could easily visit our franchisee sites and stay in close personal contact with them. Our family also enjoyed traveling to many exciting places

The journeys were not always without incident. Proof of the risk involved is a news item from the *Times-Leader* of Martins Ferry and Bellaire, Ohio, on December 19, 1972. The headline read "Slides Safely to Stop at Alderman Airport" and this story followed: *A Chicago pilot escaped injury and only minimum damage resulted to his twin-engine airplane when his landing gear failed to extend Monday while he was attempting to land at Alderman Airport, west of*

St. Clairsville. Don Hamacher put the craft down on the paved runway, swerved it into the grass as soon as he knew his wheels were still up and slid safely to a stop. Hamacher makes frequent flights into Alderman from Chicago and is associated with the Dog N Suds chain. The aircraft, a Piper Twin Comanche, had damage to the propeller and the underside of the fuselage. Once again the Hamacher luck held on or was it the skill of the pilot?

Don continues to point out the highlights of his career. *As a past president of the International Franchise Association we attended the 19th convention in Fort Lauderdale, Florida. All fifteen past presidents were awarded dark blue blazers with the IFA emblem on them. After the celebration we were invited to Bill Rosenberg's (founder of Dunkin' Donuts) home on the ocean for a big party. I remember how much I enjoyed the stone crabs.*

In 1985 Maggie and I led the Grand March for the IFA's 25th anniversary. Elmer Winters, president of Manpower, Inc., welcomed me to the stage to lead the attendees in singing. Don had written the song for the IFA celebration.

I.F.A. Celebration Song
(to the tune of 'And the Caissons Go Rolling Along')

I.F.A., I.F.A. It's the best and proper way
For a franchise to prosper and grow.
I.F.A. I.F.A. It's the best and proper way
To meet friends who are all on the go.
Twenty-five years ago all the horns did blow
That's when we started on our way.
Through thick and thin, I.F.A.'s a win.

I.F.A. is a winner today
Yes, Sir
I.F.A. is a winner today.

They liked the song and still sing it at their conventions, just changing the number of years.

Having conventions at various cities resulted in being awarded honorary titles for me. It's been fun being a Kentucky Colonel since 1968 and being made an honorary citizen of New Orleans. The city of Champaign, Illinois issued a proclamation for Jim Griggs and me to commemorate Dog N Suds Founders Day in 1998."

Along the way Don met many famous personalities whom he recalls meeting at Harvard Business School. A photograph showed Don chatting with Bud Collier, the emcee of the television show *To Tell the Truth* after Don made a promotional appearance for Dog N Suds. Other recognized names in his business life were Bob Feller, the famous baseball pitcher who keynoted the Chicago convention and Ray Nitchske of the Green Bay Packers who spoke at the 1964 Dog N Suds convention.

Without question the greatest times for Don were getting together with his business friends, Jim Griggs and John Olsen in Salt lake City in 1993, 1999, and finally in Paradise (John's hometown) in June, 2001. In their words they agreed, "Didn't we have a great time? Let's do it every year."

Thankfully memories linger and give lasting pleasure.

MY BUSINESS MEMORIES
INTERNATIONAL FRANCHISE ASSOC. 19th ANNIVERSARY
MARRIOTT HOTEL - FT. LAUDERDALE, FLORIDA - 1979

19th IFA Convention
Honors the Past,
Salutes the Future

Wearing their New IFA Blazers, 15 Past Presidents Pose for a Picture

Back row, from left: A. L. Tunick (1961), William Rosenberg (1962), Elmer Winter (1963), Grant Mauk (1964), Danaby A. Council (1966), Donald R. Hamacher (1967), Al Lapin (1968), George F. Bresnahan (1969); front row, from left: Robert M. Rosenberg (1970), Warren W. Rosenthal (1971), Ralph

Hedges (1972); Ray O. Burch (1973); Bernard S. Browning (1974); Frank L. Carney (1975); Edward Kushell (1977). Not present was Monte E. Pendleton, president in 1965. Palmer J. Wasilen, 1976 president, died Jan. 26. All were welcomed into the newly formed IFA Past Presidents' Club.

THE ASSOC. HONORED IT'S PAST PRESIDENTS WITH DARK
BLUE WOOL BLAZERS WITH THE I. F. A. EMBLEM ON THEM.
AFTER THE CELLEBRATION. WE WERE ALL INVITED OUT TO
BILL ROSENBERG,S (FOUNDER OF DUNCAN DOUGHNUTS)
HOME ON THE OCEAN FOR A BIG PARTY. I REMEMBER HOW
MUCH THAT I ENJOYED THE STONE CRABS .

MY BUSINESS MEMORIES
INTERNATIONAL FRANCHISE ASSOC. 25th ANNIVERSARY
HILTON HOTEL - FT. LAUDERDALE, FLORIDA - 1985

"I.F.A. CELEBRATION SONG"
(to the tune of "As The
Caissons Go Rolling Along")

I.F.A.   I.F.A.
It's the best and proper way
for a franchise to prosper and
grow.
I.F.A.   I.F.A.
It's the best and proper way
to meet friends who are all
on the go

Twenty-five years ago
all the horns did blow
that's when we started on our
way

Through thick and thin I.F.A.'s
a win
I.F.A. is a winner today
   YES SIR
I.F.A. is a winner today.

I WROTE THIS SONG

AND LED THE SINGING

WE LED THE GRAND MARCH

WINTERS, PRWES. OF MAN POWER
WELCOMED ME TO THE STAGE.

MY BUSINESS MEMORIES

SPOKE ON FRANCHISING AT A HARVARD BUSINESS S SEMINAR

CHATING WTTH RALPH COLLIER M.C. OF THE
TO TELL TJHE TRUTH PROGRAM

MY BUSINESS MEMORIES

IT'S BEEN FUN BEING A
KENTUCKY COLONEL
SINCE 1968

BEING MADE AN
HONORAY CITIZEN
OF
NEW ORLEANS
HAPPENDED DURING
1968 CONVENTION

RAY NITCHSKE, OF THE GREEN BAY PACKERS
SPOKE AT OUR 1964 DOG N SUDS GONVENTION

I WAS M. C. AT AN I. F. A. BANQUET
AT THE DORAL COUNTRY CLUB
IN MIAMI, FLORIDA -- 1969

BOB FELLER, BASE-BALL HERO, SPOKE
AT OUR DOG N SUDS CONVENTION
IN 1963 AT CHICAGO.

**SOME OF MY GREATEST MEMORIES
WERE THE TIMES WE GOT TOGETHER
IN SALT LAKE CITY.**

JOHN   JIM   DON

JOHN OLSEN   JIM GRIGGS   DON HAMACHER

WHAT FUN WE HAD!!
REMINISCING

CHAPTER TEN:
From Illinois to South Carolina for the Fun of It

The carefully-crafted scrapbook which chronicles the move in 1975 from Champaign, Illinois to North Myrtle Beach, South Carolina begins with this announcement in capital letters: HAMACHERS MOVE TO SOUTH CAROLINA AND MARGARET BECOMES MAGGIE, A SOUTHERN BELLE. As one turns the pages a theme emerges. The word FUN pops out on almost every page and each picture shows friends and family with wide grins taking in all that this new home has to offer. "Fun boating; fun with our dog, BeeBee; fun on the crowded beaches; fun walking along the ocean; fun playing cards on the beach are several subheadings under the many photos.

Don's words tell the story. *In 1973 we flew to Boca Raton, Florida to buy a condo for a second home. We found one and put a hold on it while we made our arrangements. On the way home we stopped in North Myrtle Beach. Gloria and Howard (Maggie's sister and brother-in-law) were there and in the process of buying a condo there. We fell in love with the area and purchased a Robbers Roost condo on first sight. We furnished it and moved in. Started flying back and forth for two years—and in September 1975 we sold our home in Champaign and moved into the Robbers Roost condo in North Myrtle Beach, South Carolina.* He also went on to explain, *In Champaign Margaret was my inspiration and she spent most of her time raising our two daughters. In North Myrtle Beach Maggie is footloose and free. We're planning on having a lot of fun times together.*

During their first year they visited a few churches and decided on the Presbyterian Church but at the same time the Lakeside Baptist minister showed up and asked Don to start a choir.at his church. As Don explains, *We both agreed to help him, but told him we would never become Baptists. When he asked me why not, I told him that I liked a cocktail before dinner and I'd heard how the southern Baptists felt about that. His quick response was that his church is a hospital for sinners, not a country club for saints. Well, I took on the choir and was surprised that the Campus Crusaders used that church as their base. Working with those wonderful young people brought me great satisfaction and their written notes to me indicated they appreciated my efforts. Their messages warmed my heart: "Don, You have a wonderful heart full of joy. I will always remember your encouragement and smiles. The Lord has used you with your gift. I really enjoyed having you as choir director. You are The Man! Thank you for the wonderful leadership executed with both passion and patience. Thank you for your joy and heart for worship". These kinds words made me love my work there.*

Finally after twenty-five years I tried to retire but the next director didn't work out so I went back for three more years until they found one that did. During those twenty-eight years at Lakeside, I took Jesus as my personal savior. Maggie used to read me stories from Hurlbert's Stories of the Bible. As she read I took notes and eventually wrote my own version of the Old Testament that I am very proud of. In 2001 we moved on to the Ocean Drive Presbyterian Church, our family denomination. Maggie and I have been blessed in so many ways. Our relationship with God is the center of our happiness." Don and Maggie were content.

On the business side, Don and Maggie both became real estate brokers with the Jackson Realty and Insurance Agency, Inc. Shortly after joining the firm, the company sponsored the Hamachers to go on a good will trip to Washington, D.C. and eastern Pennsylvania promoting North Myrtle Beach tourism. The mayor, Bryon Floyd, the city manager, Doug Wendel and several other community workers went along on the trip. The purpose was to give parties, pass out golf packages and invite vacationers to North Myrtle Beach. On the way Don and Sally Jenrette (later Sally Floyd) wrote these words to the melody of *Side by Side:*

Oh you don't have a barrel of money
To visit us down where it's sunny.
As we're travelin' along singing our song
Ya'll come on down.
We've got 29 courses for golfers,
Fishing and tennis we offer.
We've got sunbathing, too, waiting for you.
Y'all come down now.
If you're sick of the weather
Tired of the ice, sleet and snow,
You should call your family together
We've got places to go.
Now you've heard a bit of our story,
The ocean and all of its glory.
It's so easy to reach North Myrtle Beach.
Y'all come on down.

They all sang this song at the parties. Great fun and good public relations resulted in a successful venture bringing on many invasions of northerners to the Grand Strand.

Don and Maggie obviously had no trouble winning friends and influencing people. During the first ten years of their North Myrtle Beach move, they made many lasting connections. Art Coffin became Don's first boat partner and his wife, Frances, was Maggie's best friend. They took many boating trips together. Bob and Betty Lou Pitzer were their first friends and sponsored the Hamachers into the Surf Club, played lots of bridge, golf and attended Surf Club parties with them. Darrell and Justine Gunn were a fun couple. Darrell was Don's fishing buddy and golfing partner who also sang in the Grand Strand Singers under Don's direction. Don Morrell was a musician friend who recruited Don Hamacher for the Concert Board. Along with his wife Betty they had many great home parties. Frank and Nell Learnerd were their good neighbors. Frank helped everyone as the best handyman around. Monty and Ann Montgomery were a lovely couple in the neighborhood. Ann and Maggie were partners in several bridge tournaments. Pat and Margaret Murphy were a super couple who moved away. Don and Maggie visited them on Fripp Island and also in Florida. Of course, Maggie's sister Gloria and her husband Howard were part of this fun-loving circle of active friends.

Don and Maggie built a beautiful home on the Surf Club golf course across the street from Robbers Roost. Life was beautiful.

Don with two friends, Harry Bernard and Faylene Mimms, in 1978 organized a fun singing group called the North Myrtle Beach Choral Society which later became the Grand Strand Singers. They sang for many service clubs, special events, and fund-raisers. The singers worked up a popular program with a seventeen-piece dance band, performed at the high school and raised $3000 for high school band uniforms. This group sang together for twenty years.

In 1990 Don organized and directed the All-City Christmas Cantata annualy for the next 10 year. He was never far away from his love for music and performing. He served on the board of the Coastal Concert Association, the last year as president. He and Maggie enjoyed the trips to New York City to book programs for the popular cultural series. Don is a charter member of the Long Bay Symphony and served as treasurer for the first year and as president for one year. He has received many honors and recognitions for his leadership, among them he was made an honorary lifetime member of the Long Bay Symphony Board.

Another notable honor came in 2009 when Don was honored once more as the Grand Marshall of the North Myrtle Beach Christmas parade. He and Maggie riding in a convertible with one's name on the side, waving to the crowds was be quite exhilarating.

And what was Maggie up to all those years in their adopted South Carolina home? She and Martha Jackson formed a corporation to build houses, mainly as a hobby. They designed them and hired sub-contractors to do the actual construction. They did the supervising (aren't we girls good at that?) They were quite successful, clearing about $5000 on each house. Maggie did loads of volunteer work and was honored for being a top seller of Cancer Society Cookbooks from 1986 to 1989. For years she served as a board member of the Horry County Chapter of the American Cancer Society and was responsible for setting up the first annual Christmas Tour of Homes, a project that was quite successful. Maggie also played golf and bridge, drove around town in her 1969 Barracuda convertible, gave wonderful parties, planned exciting trips to exotic countries, was a P.E.O. charter member. She managed all this while making Don's active life possible and smooth. Always having fun, of course.

In 1981 the happy Hamachers built their comfortable home at 700 Holloway Circle North. Maggie edited the plans and was the contractor so under her careful and tasteful eyes, the shaded, woodsy lot became a perfect place for living and entertaining. Their new friends and neighbors enjoyed the setting as much as Don and Maggie did. Bill and Jeanette Pritchard, along with Don and Jane Preiss were their close friends. They belonged to the fun-loving group and gave some great parties at their lovely home. Jeanette was sort of the leader and she and Bill sang in the choir with Don. Clarence (another choir member) and Henrietta Belanus were another couple who loved to work on their flowers and enjoyed going on golf trips. Ed Kopriver was Don's best boat partner and super handyman. His wife Terri was a great sport on their many boat trips. Bob and Annelaise Alley were very much a part of the happy group and were skilled with computers, woodwork, and cooking. Bob and Justine Pitzer, each lost their first spouses, and later married each other. Bob was in Don's golf foursome and the couple went to the Kentucky Derby with them in 2003. Tom and Jane Staszak were great fun and gave super swim parties. Winn and Dottie Meister loved bridge and golf and were close friends of Maggie's sister and brother-in-law. Finally Art and Elinor Wieder were their close and wonderful neighbors who still watch the house faithfully when the Hamachers are on the road.

Why bother to write about past and present friends, one may ask? When looking back on life, the faces that stand out, are not only family, but also the smiling, laughing, sympathetic, helpful, understanding countenances of the many people who were and still are important parts of the long and full lives of Don and Maggie Hamacher. Would that we all were so fortunate to experience the joy of that kind of friendship and love.

FUN -- OUR THEME IN NORTH MYRTLE BEACH

FUN BOATING

FUN ON THE CROWDED BEACHES

MAGGIE & I HAVE BEEN BLESSED IN SO MANY WAYS.
OUR RELATIONSHIP WITH GOD IS THE CENTER OF OUR HAPPINESS.
I STARTED HAVING A PERSONAL RELATIONSHIP WITH GOD HERE AT LAKESIDE

Lakeside Baptist Church

PO Box 337 - Eleventh Avenue North • North Myrtle Beach, SC 29597

OUR FIRST MINISTRY WAS AT LAKESIDE BAPTIST CHURCH

1976 - DURING OUR 1st YEAR IN N. M. B. WE VISITED A FEW CHURCHES AND
HAD DECIDED ON THE PRESBYTERIAN CHURCH — HOWEVER THE LAKESIDE
MIMISTER SHOWED UP ASKED ME TO HELP THEM START A CHOIR . WE BOTH
AGREED TO HELP HIM, BUT I TOLD THAT I WOULD NEVER BECOME A BAPTIST.
WHEN HE ASKED ME - WHY NOT - I TOLD HIM THAT I LIKED A COCKTAIL BEFORE
DINNER- AND I'D HEARD HOW THE SOUTHERN BAPTISTS FELT ABOUT THAT. HIS
ANSWER WAS — OUR CHURCH IS A HOSPITAL FOR SINNERS - NOT A COUNTRY
CLUB FOR SAINTS. — WELL — I BECAME THEIR CHOIR DIRECTOR & - ACCEPTED
NO PAY - FOR 25 YRS . THEN RETIRED - BUT - THE NEXT DIRECTOR DIDN'T WORK
OUT - SO - I CAME BACK FOR 3 MORE YEARS UNTIL THEY FOUND ONE THAT DID
WORK OUT. AT THAT POINT, IN 2001 WE JOINED OUR 1st LOVE -
THE OCEAN DRIVE PRESBYTERIAN CHURCH

My choir ranged from
15 to 25 singers. During
the summer it grew to
around 70 singers.

The Campus Crusaders
used our church as their
base.Around 50 of them
sang with our choir which
gave us a big sound.
They sang with us every
summer.

HAMACHER - .HEADS CONCERT ASSOCIATION
HISTORY OF THE COASTAL CONCERT ASSOCIATOIN

In the Spring of 1971 a small group of concert lovers from Myrtle Beach and Conway organized a luncheon meeting of greater Myrtle Beach residents. The purpose was to launch a campaign to sell season tickets to a series of concerts to be performed in the new Myrtle Beach Convention Center. This campaign was immediately successful—the series was fully subscribed in just a few weeks, and thus, the Coastal Community Concert Association was begun.

For twelve years, the Association offered concerts under the aegis of the Community Concerts. In 1984 the Association went independent because the Board of Directors felt that they could offer a broader spectrum of concerts by the handling of all arrangements, programs and bookings themselves; also, the Board was fortunate enough to obtain the help of a superb musician, Donald R. Hamacher, who would personally visit the Southern Arts Federation in Atlanta and the ACCUCA in New York, (spending 3 to 5 days at each city), overseeing, previewing the performers and obtaining information concerning each group. The Association has been able to remain completely independent; henceforth, under the name Coastal Concert Association presented its first own bookings in the Fall of 1984. In this year it was also granted eleemosynary status by the State of South Carolina and the Federal government of the United States of America

by Don & Joann Wiegand

Welcome to the 14th season

of the

COASTAL CONCERT ASSOCIATION
for 1985-1986

The officers, Board of Directors and I are more than pleased to announce that again this season we have been able to schedule three free Residency Workshop Concerts for the school children to be held at 10.30 am at the Convention Center. They are as follows

Lionel Hampton Orchestra — October 2

Dance Alive (Classical ballet, contemporary & jazz) — November 12

Delphin and Romain, duo pianists — February 4

Donald R. Hamacher, President

DON & TWO FRIENDS ORGANIZE A FUN SINGING GROUP
1978 - THE N.M.B. CHORAL SOCIETY WAS FORMED
1981 - CHANGED NAME TO GRAND STRAND SINGERS

1st HARRY BERNARD then ARTHUR KENT accompanied us

THE N.M.B. CHORAL SOCIETY WAS STARTED BY FAYLENE MIMMS, A MUSIC LOVER
& GOOD ALTO WHO WORKED AT THE CHAMBER OF COMMERCE. -- HARRY BERNARD,
A GOOD TENOR, AND WAS MY CHURCH CHOIR ACCOMPANIST ---- AND MYSELF. WE
ORIGINALLY STARTED OUT WITH THE PURPOSE OF SINGING FOR OUR OWN PLEASURE.
HOWEVER, VERY SOON, WE STARTED GETTING INVITATIONS TO SING FOR VARIOUS
EVENTS AND CLUBS. WE MET EVERY MONDAY NIGHT AT THE TRINITY METHODIST
CHURCH. WE SANG RELIGIOUS, SECULAR, AND POPULAR SONGS - JUST ROR FUN, HOW-
EVER WE WORKED UP PROGRAMS FOR THE OCCASION. WE ADVERTISED AND SOON
GREW TO 40 SINGERS -- WITH SINGERS FROM MYRTLE BEACH AND AS FAR SOUTH AS
SOCASTE THIS PROMTED US TO CHANGE OUR NAME TO THE GRAND STRAND SINGERS
WE WERE SINGING 5 TO 6 GIGS PER MONTH. ---- SERVICE CLUBS--WOMEN'S CLUBS--
COMMUNITY EASTER, THANKSGIVING, & CHRISTMAS PROGRAMS--SANG OVER THE
RADIO FOR FUND DRIVES---THE HOTELS WOULD HIRE US TO GIVE 40 MINUTE PROGRAMS
AT THEIR CONVENTIONS - WE SANG AT 2 HALL OF FAME CEREMONIES -- SANG AT THE
NAT'L J.C.PENNEY CONVENTION. ONE OF OUR HIGH-LIGHTS WAS SINGING AT THE
GREATER MYRTLE BEACH ANNUAL CHAMBER OF COMMERCE BANQUET. WE SANG
FOR THE CITY XMAS-TREE LIGHTING CEREMONY EVERY YEAR.

WE WORKED UP A POPULAR PROGRAM WITH A 17 PIECE DANCE BAND
--PUT IT ON AT THE HIGH SCHOOL AS A BENEFIT TO RAISE MONEY FOR
HIGH SCHOOL BAND UNIFORMS --- WE RAISED $3000.00 FOR THEM

THE GROUP SANG TOGETHER FOR 20 YEARS

N.M.B. ALL CITY XMAS CONTATA STARTED IN 1985

HAMACHER DIRECTS ALL CITY CHRISTMAS CONTATA

Don Hamacher has been director of the North Myrtle Beach All-City Christmas Cantata Choir since its beginning nine years ago.

"For the last eight years before that I directed a group called the Grand Strand Singers," said Hamacher. "The Grand Strand Singers was about 28 singers. Three-fourths of the Grand Strand Singers still sing in this [the All-City Cantata Choir]."

Hamacher said the Grand Strand Singers sang popular songs, Golden Oldies, patriotic songs and maybe a few religious songs. He said they sang for conventions and nursing homes and for clubs all over the community.

He said Arthur Kent did some special arrangements for them and Harry Barnard played the piano. Later Barnard began singing in the chorus and Kent became accompanist.

"One year we sang for the Annual Greater Chamber of Commerce Dinner, 1,000 people down at the Landmark and one year we sang for the Hall of Fame in Myrtle Beach," said Hamacher. "The J.C. Penney Managers Convention we sang for. That was 1,000 people. We sang at the Hilton Hotel maybe 15-20

Hamacher said that one year the city approached them about singing for the Christmas festivities.

"The city came to the Grand Strand Singers and said would you come down and we'll get a piano on a truck if you need it and sing for the Christmas tree lighting?" said Hamacher. "That was [at] the old City Hall down there. That was where they used to have the Christmas tree before the Horseshoe."

He said they then began to provide the music for the annual Christmas tree lighting.

"And one time Emily Stephens, who's been on this committee [Mayor's Christmas Committee] for years, said why don't we have a program inside during this time?" said Hamacher. "I said well, that would be all right. Make it a cantata."

This agreement nine years ago was the beginning of the North Myrtle Beach All-City Christmas Cantata.

Hamacher's love of music goes back further than either of these musical groups. He was music director at McMurray College in Jacksonville, Ill., and was director of music at the high school in Champaign, Ill., when he and his wife, Maggie, permanently moved to North Myrtle Beach in 1975. He also retired at this time from his business, which he had started years

"I [also] retired from 'Dog n Suds,'" said Hamacher. "I started a chain called 'Dog n Suds.' That's hot dogs and root beer. We had 700 franchises over the country . . . 38 states."

Since his retirement and move to this area, Hamacher has directed the choir at Lakeside Baptist Church in North Myrtle Beach. He served on the board of Coastal Concert Association for five years, the last year as president. He is a charter member of the Long Bay Symphony board and served as treasurer for the first three years and later served as president for two years. Currently he is again serving as treasurer.

Hamacher and his wife live in North Myrtle Beach. They have two daughters and four granddaughters.

2008 - DON WAS AWARDED AN HONORARY LIFETIME MEMBERSHIP
IN RECOGNITION OF EXCEPTIONAL SERVICE
TO THE LONG BAY SYMPHONY

2009 - DON WAS AWARDED THE HONOR OF BEING
GRAND MARSHALL OF THE N. MYRTLE BEACH CHRISTMAS
PARADE FOR HIS LONG TIME MUSICAL
SERVICES

NEWS PAPER CLIPPINGS

W E CAME HERE TO RETIRE !!
WHAT HAPPENED ?

CHAPTER ELEVEN:
The Many Lives of Margaret (Maggie) Hamacher

By Maggie Hamacher

I, Margaret Hunter Hamacher, grew up in the small town of Paris, Missouri. My family consisted of my father, Dr. Herbert Hunter, who was a Dentist, my mother Bess, and my sister Gloria. When I was small girl, my hair was very short and blonde. I was told I looked like my dad and people called me "Little Herb"

Growing up in a little town in Missouri was an experience. The river ran through the town making for good life like jumping off a tree limb into the water or swimming back and forth hanging on to a rope and deciding not to jump or exploring caves just like Tom Sawyer.

I loved playing basketball and even though short in stature, I could outrun anyone. Because of such a small school I played on the first team and we played before the boy's game. We wore white satin outfits trimmed in blue and traveled out of town with most of Paris coming to see us play. I graduated with high honors from Paris High School in 1941. That fall I joined my sister at Missouri University. She was a year ahead of me. We stayed at Hendrex Hall, one of the larger dormitories. One day, Don sat on the porch swing and watched and decided he wanted to meet me. He said he felt sorry for the knock-kneed girl and he wanted to ask her out. (What a guy!)

The fall of my freshman year, Missouri U. won the Big 8 and so we did a snake dance through the streets of Columbia, Missouri and decided not to go to our classes. That afternoon the President of the University over the loudspeaker announced we would get a 'negative hour' if we didn't return to class. Gloriawas standing in front of Jessie Hall talking to Don after they left their Spanish Class. He "leered" at me and asked Gloria, "Is this your sister?" He then asked for a coke date. (I later found out he leered at me because he didn't have his glasses on.)

Don was like meeting a small tornado. After dating for a few years, he asked me to marry him. Being the born salesman he is, I quit school and we got married after the fall quarter on January 2, 1944. Our wedding was held at the Methodist Church in Paris, Missouri. For our honeymoon, we flew to Chicago and stayed at the Edgewater Beach Hotel which was a very exciting. We headed for Robinson, Illinois to start our marriage and his first teaching job.

Don's career in music education earned him high praise while I participated in endless community activities. I was a member of International Philanthropic Sorority Delta Theta Tau. I also volunteered for fundraising projects for the Mental Health Society, the United Fund and the Junior Women's Club. Always interested in the arts, I attended visual arts programs offered by the University of Illinois. It's easy for me to recall all the wonderful friends we made while living in Robinson, Jacksonville and Champaign. School activities, social events and civic organizations kept me busy.

In 1973, we purchased a condominium in Myrtle Beach, South Carolina for a vacation spot. After flying back and forth for 2 years, we made our move to North Myrtle Beach. At the beach I became "Maggie" a more relaxed southern name, who had never worked. I got my brokers licensed and GRI certificate and sold property for Jackson Realty Company. Martha Jackson and I build two spec homes at Cedar Creek in Little River, SC. We found the location, dreamed up the plans and hired the contractor. Later on I was the general contractor for our home at 700 Holloway Circle N. Don tried to retire, but that was a big joke.

It was not long before he had organized several singing groups and became active in several musical organizations. In 1978, the North Myrtle Beach Times labeled him, "Mr. Music Man." At my age I felt like I had had many lives:

Margaret Hunter,
    basketball star in Paris, Missouri
    Barnwarming attendant & Yearbook Savitar Queen at Missouri U
Margaret H Hamacher
    High School Music Teacher's wife in Robinson, Illinois
    MacMurray College Professor's wife Jacksonville, Illinois
    High School Music Teacher's wife in Champaign, Illinois
    President of the Dog n Suds Chain's wife
    President of the International Franchise Association's wife
    Mother of two beautiful daughters, four lovely granddaughters
    Real Estate broker in North Myrtle Beach
    And presently Don's traveling partner

Posing specific questions about life and what is important to Maggie Hamacher produced inspirational pieces of wisdom from this petite beauty with the laughing eyes. Her proudest accomplishments were her two daughters graduating from college with highest honors. Of all the travels the trip to India stood out as the most exciting mainly because she had planned all the details herself (hotels, restaurants, activities) for just the two of them. No stodgy tour group for Maggie and Don at this time. They landed in New Delhi in the middle of the night with transportation to the hotel as their first challenge. The memories gathered on that trip remain quite vivid in Maggie's mind.

Most important in Maggie's philosophy of life focuses on what she can do for others and constantly living a good Christian life. Her secret to a long marriage is to forgive and forget and have a compromising attitude. When asked about what advice she would pass on to the younger generation, her responses were quite specific: 1. Be alert to opportunities. 2. Look forward, not backward. 3. Protect your reputation. 4. Think positive. 5. Take the high road. 6. Persevere – never give up.

What a pleasure and privilege meeting and knowing Margaret Hunter Hamacher, Thank you again, Maggie

IN CHAMPAIGN MARGARET WAS ACTIVE IN
VOLUNTEER - CIVIC - AND SOCIAL ACTIVITIES

UNITED FUND
AREA CHAIRMAN

MODEL

MENTAL HEALTH ASSOC.

JR. CLUB OFFICER

DON WAS ACTIVE IN CHAMBER OF COMMERCE AND FUND DRIVES

NEW CHAMBER DIRECTORS

Hamacher UF Division 'A' Chairman

Donald R. Hamacher, president of Dog 'n Suds, Inc., will lead the United Fund's "A" division for this year's fund campaign.

Hamacher will head all large Champaign-Urbana businesses in the upcoming campaign in an all-out effort to meet the division goal of $141,200.

HAMACHER He is first vice president of the International Franchise Association, president of Champaign High School's Music Parents Club, director of Champaign First Methodist Church's Youth Choir, and a member of Kiwanis and Champaign Chamber of

Hamacher 1st Dining Hall 'Salesman'

Don Hamacher, president of Dog 'n Suds, Inc., has volunteered as the first "salesman" in the Arrowhead Boy Scout Council's campaign to "sell" the idea of constructing a new dining hall at Camp Drake.

The sales campaign, a unique fund-raising venture construct a replacement for the ancient hall now in use at Camp Drake offers all area salesmen a chance to "sell" the dining hall to the community.

HAMACHER

The sales campaign will be May 2 through 22 beginning with at 7:30 p.m. kickoff dinner in the Urbana Lincoln Sidewalk Cafe.

According to Tom Jones, approximately 150 volunteer salesmen are expected to attend the dinner, where they will receive final assignments of five persons to contact in their selling.

Chapter Twelve:
Have Plane, Will Travel

To say there is a definite advantage in being a relative, friend, or acquaintance of Don and Maggie Hamacher is a huge understatement. If one has a wanderlust or a need to travel to a reasonably accessible location, they are your means of getting there and having a great time at any destination. Their travelogue before moving to North Myrtle Beach in 1975 reads like a National Geographic Magazine focused on Memorable Places for Family and Friends. Add in the fact that Don owned an impressive series of airplanes—the last one was a twin engine Comanche—and a lifetime of globetrotting results.

Grab your backpack and enjoy the Hamacher travel experiences.

When they were first married, Canada was the destination where they actually made a surfboard because there was nowhere to buy one. On a trip to Key Lake, Wisconsin they rented a quaint cottage and the whole family went horseback riding. During one ride they were attacked by a swarm of bees which caused everyone but Don to head back quickly. An hour later he returned, covered with red welts, in agony and in his words "fit to be tied".

Don's advice for travelers was not always reliable. A prime example of this shortcoming occurred on a pre-planned journey to Gatlinburg with their two daughters and the Smith family, Don flew in from a business trip, while the others motored in from Illinois to join him. He arrived early and called to suggest that they pack warm clothes for the vacation. Don failed to notice that he was waiting for them in an air-conditioned room. The actual temperature outside hit 90+ degrees and it was "hotter than heck" (his words) when they arrived. The automobile travelers never let him forget his slight weather mistake.

Don and Maggie took the girls to Europe for three adventurous weeks. In Paris they discovered the best onion soup available in the Underground at night. Don relied on "the point book" to communicate and get what he wanted. Attempting to get a snack for the family at a food shop across the street from their hotel, he tried to speak the language. He wanted some good cheese and was really asking for "kind cheese" in French. The merchant did not understand and finally Diane, who was studying the language in school, came and succeeded in buying the desired cheese. This incident convinced Don to stick with just pointing to the picture in his book in order to get his point across.

Florida was a frequent destination for Don for business and family flights. One challenging trip occurred when Don and Maggie flew their two daughters who were married within three months of each other and their new husbands to Florida (total six) in his four-space plane. He adapted the space by pre-shipping the luggage, eliminating one gas tank to cut down the weight, and adding two extra seat belts. They stopped in Nashville and Jacksonville for gas and everyone arrived safely and happy.

Don recalled one other business trip when he volunteered to pick up a colleague, Paul Lewis, in Greenwood, Indiana near Indianapolis. Paul commented that he was not afraid to die but he didn't want to go when it was Don's time to expire.

On a business/pleasure flight to Tampa, Maggie took her sewing machine with her to occupy her time. Constant rain pelted the city so when Don discovered that the weather was good in Nassau, the adventuresome couple decided to land there. Since they had to declare all possessions before entering the British island, the sewing machine surprised the customs staff. They stated that it was an odd item to take on vacation. Maggie was happy, so nothing else mattered.

Don and Maggie took their daughters on many amazing trips. The family flew to the Grand Canyon, to ski sites in Michigan and Colorado, to the lovely Mackinaw Island where they had to land off island because no vehicles are permitted there. Big Ten football games, the Rose Bowl, Shawnee on the Delaware, Callaway Gardens in Alabama, and twice to the The Broadmoor in Colorado. Those were among their favorites.

All journeys were not always 'up in the air' for the Hamachers and their companions. Sailing was another passion. Don and Jan Jackson, Don's cousin, inspired and accompanied them to the Abacos, a group of five islands where they sailed three different times. Another favorite venture was sailing through the British Virgin Islands. Maggie even wrote a song about this adventure:

SAILING, SAILING
(Maggie's words to this melody)
Sailing, sailing without a sense of fear,
Four cousins started out to sea
With groceries and their beer.

Dingy, dingy. That's how we go to shore
With Jackson as our captain,
Who could ask for more?

Jana, Jana, Knew how to catch with hook,
The mooring buoys in the sea
She did it by the book.
Hamacher, Hamacher, he always cooked our meals
And in between, the cards came out.
Now wasn't that a deal?

Maggie, Maggie, happy to be along.
She spotted buoys near the shore
And wrote this sailing song.
Cigaro, Cigaro that was the ship's full name,
With these two sails a-flying high,
That's how we came to fame.

Windy, rainy, our weather came and went,
With blessings from the Lord above,
The sun was finally sent.
Sailing, sailing, around the BVI's
The seven days went mighty fast,
Our memories were the prize.

When they were not flying or sailing to tropical destinations, Don
and Maggie loved the Big Apple as well for the theater, shopping,
and atmosphere. A really wonderful stay at the famous Waldorf
Astoria in New York City provided an amazing accidental meeting
with the president of Gulf State Paper. This company supplied paper
goods to Dog N Suds, the company that Don and Jim founded. Don

met the gentleman who happened to be on crutches resulting from a horse jumping incident. During a chat in the bar Don mentioned that he and Maggie wanted to buy new collars for their dogs, Dolly and Fanny. Asking about where they might find a store in the city, the man directed them to a business at Rockefeller Center that sells everything. He had just bought a bell at this place for a recently purchased church that he had moved to his property in Mississippi. (Doesn't everyone have a church placed on their land?) Don and Maggie did find the perfect collars for their pets at the boutique his new acquaintance suggested. This chance meeting lead to visits on the company Lear jet to Gulfport, Mississippi as a customer perk. Sometimes it pays to talk to strangers in bars. They eventually become valuable friends.

Journeys to many other exotic lands included Portugal where he bought Maggie beautiful twenty-three carat gold bracelets now housed in the bank box. In Spain on the Algarvi Coast they stayed in a high rise hotel surrounded by a soft sandy beach. Ever the romantic, Don drew a large heart in the sand below. When Maggie looked down she saw this and the sweet message 'I love you' written for her.

They sailed the Greek Islands with a group from Illinois University. In Rhodes Don took an empty wine bottle to a vineyard where they filled it up for a grand total of fifteen cents. He was sorry he had only brought one bottle!

Now prepare for some serious travel with Don and Maggie.

DON LOGGED OVER 6000 HOURS IN THIS PLANE BUILDING THE DOG N SUDS CHAIN TO 650 FRANCHISED DRIVE INS.

CHAPTER THIRTEEN:
Back to Churchill Downs

April 2011 is here and Maggie and I are preparing for the annual pilgrimage to the Kentucky Derby, a journey we have made for the past fifty-two years. This adventure began when Bob Gupton, a Dog N Suds operator and good friend, invited us to join him in the box he had at the Derby. The winner that initial year was Decidedly and we were privileged in 1973 to see Secretariat triumph and go on to win the Triple Crown. For the first twenty-five years the Gupton's friends, Kenny and Juanita Marshall joined us in the box and we all stayed at the Gupton home. Naturally, they were gracious, southern hosts.

Don excitedly describes the annual pilgrimage to Kentucky. *After the first year we could bring friends and of course we asked our favorite traveling companions Bob and Chris Smith to join us. We all flew to the Derby in our trusty Comanche every year until 1994 when our dear friend Bob Gupton died and Maggie didn't want to fly anymore. From then on we drove each year enjoying the beautiful scenery from North Myrtle Beach, through the North Carolina mountain country, the Tennessee countryside, then the welcoming fields of Kentucky. In that year Maggie and I began a new tradition. We stayed at the Gold Vault Hotel* in Radcliffe, Kentucky, twenty-nine miles south of Louisville near Fort Knox. For the past seventeen years Maggie and I have been comfortable in the same room #129. Our door opens to a long pool, an inviting hot tub, and an atrium where we all meet to talk about our betting strategies for the race. In 1994, that infamous year of change, I was able to buy a box at the Derby. This purchase included tickets for the Oak Day races on Friday so we always sold those to Bob's nephew Larry Gupton. Everyone seemed happy with that arrangement. After this year of 2011 boxes will be available to club members at $4000 annually and must be applied for via email. I suppose change is a good thing.

Our Derby experiences are somewhat of a ritual and we savor each step of our stay. We do have our favorite places to visit and dine. On Friday mornings we often visit one of the distilleries—either Jim Beam or Makers Mark. The tastings are quite pleasant. At noon we have a wonderful lunch at the classy Captains Quarters on the Ohio River. In the earliest years we had Friday dinners at the famous Koontz Supper Club in downtown Louisville. The waiting line for this famous eatery usually stretched a full city block but Bob Gupton knew the manager who always led us to the front. I'm sure this did not sit well with the observers but we followed our leader willingly. After the Gault House Hotel was built downtown on the river, we enjoyed Friday night dinners and the exceptional views at the revolving Rainbow Supper Club at the top of the hotel. One Friday afternoon we took a boat ride on the Louisville Riverboat. I bought a captain's hat, wore it all evening at the Gault and was amazed by the excellent service extended to our group. Was it really the hat or just the superior staff?

Early in the morning of the Derby Maggie and I love to go to Weidners, a restaurant on the far side of Churchill Downs where the jockeys gather for breakfast. Visiting the paddocks is also a high point of Derby Day. Bob used to give corsages to the ladies and black ties to the men in the days when dress was rather formal. Times as they say have changed drastically even *at the Derby. When the ladies stop wearing the elaborate hats, an era of gentility will be gone but the race will go on forever.*

Some traditions never change, however. The ten-dollar mint juleps are always delicious and go quite well with the sandwiches we bring with us. My betting strategy of putting $2.00 to $5.00 on the favorite horse to show continues to keep me excited. Some habits are hard to break. My wagering system fails when the favorites come in fourth and all is lost. Some day in the future I may figure out how to bet on a sure thing. We are such big players, aren't we?

Fifty-two years at the Kentucky Derby have been a highlight of our lives and we are not done yet. Lest you worry about the drive, please know that our daughter Diane will be accompanying us and will enjoy the festivities with us.

AND WE'RE OFF AND RUNNING!

KENTUCKY DERBY

1960
The beginning group for 34 yrs.

1993
N. Myrtle Bch. friends joined us

2011 - Ladies hats were still important

2011 group eating at Doe Run Inn

CHAPTER FOURTEEN:
Seeing Our World with Don and Maggie

Pack your imagination, your sense of adventure and a desire to extend your boundaries. We are about to travel vicariously to several continents, countries, cities and cultures with Don and Maggie Hamacher who have seen it all and then some. Our journeys will be relaxing because our hosts have done all the hard work connected with planning the details, recording their experiences and, best of all, sharing the highlights with us. We are not even required to pack our passports, toothbrushes, comfortable shoes or American Express card. Simply sit back and enjoy Africa, Turkey, Egypt, and India through the keen senses of seasoned travelers whose mission is to live life to the fullest. Get a good night's sleep. We'll be in Africa in the morning.

The year is 1994. Capetown, an amazing metropolis, welcomes us to South Africa with open arms. We enjoy our first breakfast at Squares. The brochure describes it as "an upbeat designer restaurant flocked to by the 'in-crowd' for the city-centre breakfast, snack or lunch. Now that the adjacent mall is paved and traffic-free, the ambiance is wonderfully cosmopolitan." The hotel proves convenient to shopping. The St. George Street Mall, a flea market directly across from our hotel and the bank's foreign exchange department are a must. Waterfront cruises, free Sunday concerts, street performers, great eateries kept us happy. We ordered eighteen carat gold enhancers for blue topaz stones for our four granddaughters from the Capetown goldsmiths. As true tourists we took the Cape Point Tour which earned us a certificate which reads "This certifies that Don and Maggie have stood at the tip of Africa, where the Atlantic and Indian Oceans meet, where the Trade Routes of the East and the West cross, where the Legend of the Flying Dutchman still lives and which 'Discoverer', Sir Francis Drake called *The Fairest Cape we saw in the whole circumference of the Globe.* We also viewed the Hottentots Mountains—Hottentots is Dutch for 'stuttering'.

The wine country tour included KWV Cellars, the Franschoek Vineyards at Boschendal the home of the French Huguenots. Of interest—rosebushes are planted at the end of each row of grapes to take care of bugs. Hmm—I wonder how well that works. Google will know.

We move on to Johannesburg, a city brought into being by gold. "The chance of making big money has attracted people the City of Gold since the early shanty town days. Many of those with initiative and drive have succeeded. Baronial mansions in the 'mink and manure belt', their grounds lined with tennis courts and fleets of Ferraris testify to the fact that Jo-burg, at the top of the supertax bracket, is a very affluent society. This is a high voltage nouveau riche territory—fast-paced, fun. Superb hotels, restaurants and shopping centers pander to those with five-star tastes. Golf courses, botanical gardens and parks are dotted about among the high-rise buildings, and the immaculately manicured gardens of the northern suburbs are worth a leisurely drive. Suggested activities from the guide include sensational views from the top of the Ritz-Carlton, hot air balloon rides, stargazing at the Planetarium, rowing boats on Zoo Lake. Johannesburg also is within easy flying or driving distance of untamed Africa and some of the country's finest game reserves.

We stay at the elegant Balalaika Protea Hotel in Sandton, a suburb of Jo-burg. From there we to move on Gold Reef City, enjoy Zulu dancers performing, descend a gold mine which is not for claustrophobics.

At last we discover the real heart of the dark continent—Harry's Camp, part of the Mala Mala Game Reserve. Our guide meets us at the Skukuza Airport and the adventure begins when we see warthogs running in the front yard of the camp. On our safaris in a trusty Land Rover we see them all: elephants, leopards, buffalo, rhinoceros, hyenas, zebras, giraffes, hippos, lions, white rhinos, and those cute little warthogs.

The true highlight of our African trip in 1994 was the celebration of Don and Maggie's fiftieth wedding anniversary. Congratulations and fortunately, they are still enjoying their life together today in 2011 and what a life it is!

DON AND MAGGIE'S
WE ENJOYED OUR **50th ANNIVERSARY** AT CAPE POINT

Where the Indian and Atlantic ocean meet.

CAPE POINT
SOUTH AFRICA

THIS CERTIFIES THAT
DON and MAGGIE
has stood at the tip of Africa,
where the Atlantic and Indian Oceans meet,
where the Trade Routes of the East and West cross
where the Legend of the Flying Dutchman still
lives and which, Discoverer,
Sir Francis Drake called
"The Fairest Cape we saw in the whole
circumference of the Globe."

CAPE POINT

A romantic Southern African holiday

PIANIST SANG ANNIVERSARY SONG

ESPECIALLY FOR US

SINGING HAPPY ANNIVERSARY

VILLIERA TRADITION CHAMPAGNE

WHILE IN AFRICA WE VISITED
HARRY'S SAFARI LODGE

WE SAW THE BIG FIVE
ON OUR FIRST HUNT

1. ELEPHANT 3. BUFFALO
2. LEOPARD   4. LION
              5. RHINO

VIEWING OUR 1ST ELEPHANT

DON REACHED OVER & SAID
TO MAGGIE, " WE'RE HAVING THE
THE TIME OF OUR LIVES, ARE'NT WE?"

THE LEOPARDS MOVED AT A FAST PACE, WE
KNOCKED DOWN TREES ETC. TO KEEP UP

SURROUNDED BY BUFFALO HERD

TRIBE OF LIONS ASLEEP LATE AFTERNOON
A LIONS ROAR CAN BE HEARD 5 MILES AWAY

RHINO

CHAPTER FIFTEEN:
Adventure, Anyone?

It's October 1992. Don and Maggie are heading to Turkey and they're taking us along. The journey starts in Istanbul and we are staying at the best hotels which is a definite bonus as we enter a world of ancient civilizations, magnificent culture, and stunning beauty. This city is billed as "The Exotic Empress of the World" Our guides tell us that they had to invent a special word to describe Instanbul: Byzantine. Byzantium sits at the juncture of the Marmara, Bosphorus, and Golden Horn—the crossroads of Europe and Asia. For 1000 years it was a bejeweled metropolis where Constantine, Justinian, and Suliman the Magnificent displayed booty gathered from Jerusalem to the very gates of Vienna. An infinite variety of museums, ancient churches, palaces, great mosques, bazaars are there to explore. Maggie describes the experience as stepping into a living history book. The Blue Mosque famous for its blue tiles with its six magnificent minarets is especially impressive at night The Bosphorus is eighteen miles long and only passage from the Black Sea to the Mediterranean Sea. On our cruise of the legendary strait we marvel at the imperial palaces and fortresses, cafes and restaurants all along the shores.

Other highlights on the tour were seeing Don Hamacher in a red fez hat, the gypsies with the trained brown bears, and the satin outfits that Turkish boys wear for their circumcisions. The harem favorite room and the elaborate harem baths in the Topkapi Palace were breathtaking. We knew we were not in South Carolina anymore. Shopping at the Grand Bazaar was one of the delights of visiting Istanbul. There are 4,000 shops—goldsmith streets, carpet streets, leather streets ad infinitum—a shopper's paradise.

We board the Turkish Airlines for the flight to Izmir, Turkey's third largest city, Smryna of old. The spectacular ruins of Ephesus and Pergamum and two of the ancient Seven Churches of Asia Minor are historic treasures in this city. Of interest is the fact that Izmir is the southeastern headquarters of NATO.

Turkish desserts are delicious and rich. Many are baked, such as crumpets, cookies or shredded wheat, all in syrup. *Baklava* comes in several varieties: *cevisli* is with chopped walnut stuffing, *fistikli* is with pistachios, *kaymikli* is with clotted cream. Turkish fruits offer a perfect alternative to sweet desserts. We must try *kavun*, a sweet melon or *karpuz*, a variety of watermelon.

Our time in Izmir would not be complete without a march of protestors after a funeral of a soldier who was shot by a sniper. This brings us back to the reality of the modern world.

We travel on to Ephesus and walk the Marble Road to the great ruins as they did 2000 years ago. The Virgin Mary and St. Paul both lived for a time in Ephesus. The Gospel first was preached in Turkey. The Holy Roman Empire advanced here. Hannibal, Julius Caesar, and Alexander the Great all fought here. How's that for dropping a few names to impress you?

En route to Antalya, the jewel of Turkey's Turquoise Coast,

we dip our toes into the medicinal hot spring waters at Pamukkle. The amazing "frozen waterfalls", the calcareous water cascades and drips crystallized into dazzling white stalactites, were an amazing, unforgettable adventure. Another memorable sight in Pamukkle was seeing Don on the receiving end of a camel kiss. He gathered admirers wherever he went.

From camels in Pamukke to belly dancers in Antalya on the Meditarranean coast was a surprisingly smooth transition. Here we marveled at the fluted minaret, the old clock tower, the statue of Ataturk who was the founder of the Republic of Turkey. At the Antalya Museum we saw artifacts dating from the Stone Ages through the Helenistic periods to the modern era. Along the road cotton farmers line their full wagons up waiting sometimes two or three weeks to have their harvested crop weighed. Other typical scenes were women in fields picking sesame seed and potatoes. Where would the progress of civilizations be without the feminine work ethic?

On to the heart of Turkey, Central Anatolia, and Cappadocia where we explored the Valley of Goreme, a lunar landscape sculpted by the wind, water and volcanic ash—unlike anything we've ever seen. Early Christians sheltered here in cones and chimneys built into the rock, in underground chambers, churches, entire villages some fourteen stories deep. We learn here that Anatolia was the first stronghold of Christianity. The Fresco of St. Helena, mother of Constantine the Great, is found in the Church beneath the Tree in Cappadochia. . This area is also known for its fine grapes which are fertilized from pigeon droppings and volcanic ash. No wonder the wine is so delicious.

The sculpture of three women, one representing peace, the middle figure is crying mourning the Ataturk's death in 1938, the third depicts modern women is a striking work of art in front of

Ataturk's mausoleum in Ankara. This capital city offers museums, restaurants, lodging that equals any warm and exciting metropolis we have visited.

We cannot leave Turkey without additional little known facts about this marvelous country. Did you know that (1) Turkey is a secular democratic republic since 1952? (2) The sites of Troy, Pergamum, Aphrodisias, and Antioch still stand there? (3) Homer, Herodotus, Galen, Santa Claus, St. Paul, and Midas were born here? (4) Turkish women earned the right to vote in 1934 and within two years were serving in parliament? (5) Three of the Seven Wonders of the World stood here. Ephesus' Temple of Artemis, Mausolus' Tomb at Halicayrnassus, and the Collossus of Rhodes—all part of Turkey until 1947? And (6) The Ottoman Empire stretched from Persia across North Africa to the very gates of Vienna?

I cannot resist passing on some truly exotic facts. "Noah landed his ark here…Ulysses led a host of heroes to its Aegean shores…the patriarch of Abraham shepherded his tribe across its southern area… St. Paul spread the gospel throughout…St. John and the Virgin Mary retired here (separately?)…Caesar came, saw and conquered." Modern connoisseurs love Turkey for its contemporary attractions, five-star hotels and divine cuisine. Beaches are as unspoiled as they were when Anthony and Cleopatra honeymooned there. That is certainly something provocative to think about as we depart this incredible land.

TURKEY
INCREDABLE --- UNFORGETABLE
LIKE STEPPING INTO A LIVING HISTORY BOOK

FAMOUS BLUE MOPSQUE AND IT'S 6 MINARETS

ISTANBUL
THE EXOTIC "EMPRESS OF THE WORLD"

Elaborate. Mysterious. Sumptuous. They had to invent a special word to describe Istanbul: *Byzantine*. Byzantium of old sits at the juncture of the Marmara, Bosphorus, and Golden Horn — the crossroads of Europe and Asia — and for 1000 years it was a bejeweled metropolis where Constantine, Justinian, Suleyman the Magnificent and others displayed booty from Jerusalem to the very gates of Vienna. Much of it is still there for you to explore!

Don gets a kiss from the camel

Travel back almost 2000 years as you walk the Marble Road to the great ruins at Ephesus.

127

The Heart of TURKEY Central Anatolia
CAPPADOCIA

GÖREME

These 1000 yr. old Rock Homes were occupied until recently

KLI

Christians , in hiding, occupied these
caves, often called Under-ground citys.
Some were 8 floors deep with ventilation.

Maggie is looking into a
caved Christian church.

CHAPTER SIXTEEN:

Passage to India

Before we board the plane that takes us to the other side of the world with the Hamacher Dynamic Duo, it is important to know a fact that makes this trip unique. Maggie is the chief travel agent for this journey. No ordinary group tours are built into this adventure. This journey is designed for just the happy couple so we are tagging along this time for the sheer excitement. Certainly there are surprises in store in this land of startling contrasts.

First we fly to Frankfurt, Germany and stop briefly at the Wings Hotel. It is the first Saturday after Thanksgiving, 1995 and we have some time to take the subway into town to enjoy the food, beer, hot wine, festivities offered by this hospitable place. We have our fill of the German treats and are ready to head to Delhi, the capital of India. A slight problem arises upon landing: it is the middle of the night and no immediate transportation to the Ambassador Hotel is available. Don, ever the salesman, manages to find a nocturnal driver willing to deliver the weary travelers to their first Indian lodging. Imagine the fare for that small favor!

The typical crowded streets of Delhi, the many scooter rickshaws, the presence of turbaned, well-educated Sikhs (who never cut their hair) introduce us to the strange, exotic atmosphere of Indian life and culture.

One of the first stops in New Delhi is the American Embassy to register our itinerary for safety precautions, then on to the Indian Tourist Office for information. Of interest is the fact that our taxi driver left us out at the wrong place and we had to walk four long blocks to the embassy. Hmmm.

The Jami Masjid, the largest mosque in India, requested that we climb 122 steps, leave our shoes at the entrance and join worshippers in the huge building. This mosque can hold 20,000 devotees and have individual places to lie down for prayer. Also in Delhi we encountered many beggars and snake charmers outside the Red Fort, the fascinating palace-citadel of Emperor Shahjahan once studded with precious stones and painted with gold. On to Raj Ghat, the peaceful and green memorial to the Father of the Nation, Mahatma Ghandi. In New Delhi, labeled the city of the great Mughals and the gateway to the Golden Triangle, the famous Hindu Temple contains all seven deities of the Hindu Pantheon as well as paintings of the Sikh gurus and Jesus Christ. The scope of this religious site was eye opening. The Crafts Museum was designed like a real Indian village where artisans created beautiful handicrafts as we admired their skills. Don bought Maggie a hand-woven accent rug here.

Our next city of India was Varanasi where the crazy traffic kept our bicycle rickshaw driver Ompaca on the alert. We made him our permanent driver during our stay here. Here traffic stops for wandering cows and other cyclists. We spent much of our time in heavy traffic with our eyes closed.

We arose very early for a 5:30 boat tour on the Holy Ganges River where Hindu pilgrims flock to the banks to do their gymnastic exercises and have a ritual bath. All who labor and are heavily laden go there to wash away their sins. One guide stated the ways to get benefit from the Ganges is to see the river, bathe in the waters and drink this holy water. Add to that knowledge is the fact that when someone dies, he is immediately cremated and the ashes strewn into the Ganges trusting that he will then be sure of a better life in his reincarnation. Our guide on the boat ride, Ashok is also on the radio and is a manager of a nursery to third grade school. His name means happy ma. St. Thomas traveled to India and was credited for the Christian movement there. The Beneres (Hindu) University educates medical and art students from South Africa, England and America. There is a separate college for women. Arranged marriages are still existent in the Indian culture.

The flight to Agra never took place because of a blown tire after a hard landing at Khahurano. The airport manager had to find ways to get the rest of the passengers to Agra. He furnished a bus for tour groups and a taxi for us—and a free dinner. The eight hour taxi ride over hazardous roads was, in Maggie's words, a nightmare. Road tea stops along the road helped our driver stay alert and warm since he had worked the dayshift already and it was very cold that night.

Agra is the city of the inimitable Taj Mahal, one of the Seven Wonders of the World, and exceeded all expectations. We viewed it at sunrise. The pure white marble gleamed as we viewed the most elaborate tomb ever erected by the fifth Mogul Emporer Shahjehan in memory of his beloved wife, Mumtaz who died in 1631. We were also impressed with the Agra Red Fort where Mughal emperors ruled India for a century from this place.

Although reluctant to leave this beautiful city we forged on to Jaipur where our scooter rickshaw broke down on the way to the Ashkok Hotel. We dismissed that driver and the guide as we were not very pleased with them. The friendly staff at the hotel made up for this mild disappointment. Again Don posed wearing a maharajah's headdress at the Rajasthan Government of India Handcraft Shop. He can be quite a ham when he wants. The Peacock Entrance to the present Maharanja's palace is breathtaking. When a flag is waving, the maharajah is at home. Another site The Amber Palace, the former capitol of the royals, can be reached on foot, or by paying to go in a Jeep, or by elephant for 200 rupees apiece. We chose the elephant of course. Being in the Maharajah's bedroom with the chamber of mirrors was well worth it. From the elephant ride back we saw saffron, a costly spice and food coloring, being grown.

Our final leg of the trip is Udaipur, the White City of lakes, probably one of the most beautiful cities in India. Udaipur's founder the maharajah Udai Singh had polio and his palace had a cupola where he sat to view the wonders of his city. Puppet show performances, art schools, boat rides on Lake Pichola gave us lovely memories of this special city. The James Bond movie *Octopussy* was filmed at our hotel and on Jag Mandir Island. We can always revisit those beautiful locations watching re-runs of that picture.

After a magical month of exploration in India, we head home to our relaxing bungalow in North Myrtle Beach, greeted by our good friends who are happy to welcome home the weary travelers. Maggie did a superb job as the travel agent for the India trip. She may have missed her calling.

INDIA - A MUCH DIFFERENT CULTURE

NEW DELHI - VARANASAI - AGRA
JAIPUR & UDAIPUR

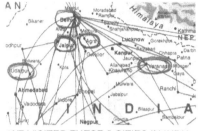

WE VISITED THESE 5 CITIES IN INDIA

CRAZY TRAFFIC IN NEW DELHI

HARD TO FIND A TAXI AT 2pm
WE FELT SOMEWHAT UNEASY

ALL TRAFFIC STOPS FOR WANDERING COWS

INDIA - A FACINATING COUNTRY

THE SACRED GANGES RIVER
RUNS THROUGH VARANASI

A RICKSHAW TAXI IN AGRA

WE RODE AN ELEPHANT UP TO
THE AMBER PALACE IN JAIPUR

THE BEAUTIFUL **TAJ MAHAL** -
YOU MUST SEE IT TO BELIEVE IT.

OUR HOTEL ON THE LAKE IN UDAIPUR
HAD A BEAUTIFUL SETTING

A SNAKE CHARMER

CHAPTER SEVENTEEN:

Visiting King Tut, His Land and His Friends

A news headline dated March 9, 2005 read "Recent CT scans on Tut's mummy rule out violence". The story revealed the details: Zahi Hawass, the head of the Egyptian Supreme council for Antiquities said that the results of the scan on 3,300-year-old mummy of King Tutankhamen indicate that he was not murdered but may have suffered a badly broken leg shortly before his death. This was probably positive news for the land and people of Egypt and an interesting fact for Don and Maggie who had toured this fascinating country in October 1997. As usual they shared their visit with us via their thoroughly written records of that trip and as usual we learned a great deal about the country, the sights, and the people.

Egypt is located in the northeastern corner of Africa and covers an area of 386,000 square miles. Only about 5% of the country is inhabited along the banks of the Nile whose course stretches over 900 miles from the Mediterranean to the north and the Sudan in the south. To the west lies Libya and to the east are the desert plateau, Red Sea and the Sinai. Egypt's most fertile area is the Nile Delta. Cairo, Egypt's capital has 14 million inhabitants and Alexandria, the second largest city, has a population of 5.5 million. Egypt's total population is 60 million. About 90% are concentrated in the fertile Nile Delta and live in 5% of the country's territory. In the 90's there has been an urban migration. The people are outgoing, warm and have a distinct sense of humor. They have respect and a liking for foreigners, and a deep sense of tolerance for other races, religions and nationalities. The source of this description was obviously from a travel brochure from the 1990's. Much has happened in Egypt in the most recent years. It would be extremely interesting to update the position and outlook of this ancient country and its people today. The leadership and economic situation in the Middle East has changed drastically.

The Hamachers stayed at the Cairo Marriott Hotel and Casino which was formerly the old Gezira Palace built in 1869 for Princess Eugenia used for the Suez Canal opening. In this city there is lots of ground to cover so the taxi drivers outside the hotel bargained for hire for any trip we wanted to take. They seemed to enjoy Don's company. Even our favorite waiter Waheed at the hotel said "I feel something very strong in my heart for you". We felt honored.

The Great Pyramid, some say the most famous structure in the world, was built by King Cheops of the fourt dynasty in 2650 B.C. Almost 2.5 million blocks of stone were put into building this pyramid. Close to the eastern flank of the Pyramid of Cheops lie three small pyramids dedicated either to his wives or family members. We dutifully climbed the steps to the entrance to the tomb. At times we crouched, climbed steep and dark stairways and squeezed into small spaces to reach the burial chambers. When the passage got harder we wondered whether it was worth it and began to dread the way back to the outside.

We cannot miss the Sphinx, the legendary monument carved from the outcrop of soft limestone that was supposedly left standing after the harder surrounding stone was quarried for the Great Pyramid. Conventional archaeology credits Chephren, Cheop's son, with the idea of shaping it into a figure with a lion's body and a human head which is often identified as his own, complete with royal beard and uraeus.

We were driven around by our favorite driver Khaleed in a comfortable Mercedes and employed a wonderful guide, Dahlia. He took us to Coptic Cairo where the Alabaster Pulpit with its thirteen pillars representing Jesus and his disciples. One of the pillars is black for Judas. According to the Coptic tradition, Christianity was brought to Egypt by Saint Mark who arrived in the time of Nero. St. Mark converted many to the new underground faith, founding the Patriarchate of Alexandria in 61 AD. The Al-Mu'allaqah Church or Hanging Church dates back to the 4th or 5th century and houses a painting of Mary and Baby Jesus, often called "The Egyptian Mona Lisa". In the Church of Abu Sergah (St. Sergius) is the cave where the Holy Family stayed when they fled to Egypt to escape King Herod.

Dahlia took them to the Egyptian Museum, a somewhat ponderous sandstone neoclassical building originally called the Cairo Museum, which opened in 1902. In the forecourt are ancient statues which would be protected prizes elsewhere in the world, but here they are exposed to enhance fully the drama of the entrance. This museum houses upwards of 100,000 objects, only a tiny fragment of which can be exhibited at any one time. The treasures are displayed in chronological order that enables us to follow the evolution of Egyptian civilization. Don and Maggie liked this tour so well that they went back on their own. They loved the gilded wooden statue of Tutankhamen standing in a boat posing with a spear, the wooden statue of Anubis sitting on his shrine, and many treasures only seen in art books and magazines that hardly do their beauty justice.

The shopping in Cairo is another fine adventure. Don purchased gifts for his girls: eighteen carat gold hand made double cartouches, an aquamarine pendant, some silver boxes, and six eighteen carat gold chains. He loves to make the Hamacher women happy.

The Nile River cruise on the H.S. Radamis was another high point. The cabins on board were spacious and even had private facilities with a bathtub. We flew from Cairo to Luxor to begin the cruise. We also got acquainted with our new guide, Ismael, and our fellow cruise people at the East Bank of Luxor. At one time there were 5,000 sphinxes lining the streets from Karnak to Luxor Temple. Here we were in awe of the immense columns of Karnak's Temple built over 2,000 years ago. Each pharaoh added his own contribution. The notorious Ramses II lived the longest and had one hundred wives. That rascal! His colossal statue with one of his daughters guards the entrance to the Second Pylon of the temple. (I wonder how many children he had!) By the way, the Luxor Temple at night was spectacular.

The Valley of the Kings and Queens was another source for royal namedroppers: Ramses II's father's tomb, Queen Hatshepsut, Tutankhamen, Nefertiti, the God Horus, the Goddess Isis—to mention a few celebrities. Incidentally, an outdoor presentation of the opera Aida was performed at the Queen's temple. This must have been incredible.

Meanwhile, back to the Nile cruise where several new interesting friendships were formed. Most elegant was Genevieve, a dress designer from France now living in South Africa and her friend Richard, a CPA from Johannesburg. We celebrated Richard's fifty-first birthday on board topping a lovely dinner and a luscious cake with a toast of Le Grande Dame champagne for $150 per bottle purchased by Genevieve, of course.

The last night on the cruise ship was also festive and unforgettable.

We left the ship at the Aswan area and toured the granite quarries site of the unfinished 1,170 ton obelisk. Don gathered pieces of quarried stones which he handed out to all on the bus ride to the Philae, the Temple of Isis. Quite honestly, he was thinking of selling them. There's that "He can sell anything" trait again.

In Cairo we loved the zoo and both Don and Maggie held and cuddled a twenty-one day old baby lion. We knew that in another month that darling little kitty could take quite a nip out of our skin.

Other Cairo highlights included the riverboat restaurants, the belly dancers, and the tasty international food. We did take precautionary medicines in case unpleasant gastric episodes occurred. Never forget the Pepto-Bismol for mild upsets, the Larium for malaria, the Imodium for diarrhea, tetanus shots for whatever can happen and the ever-reliable flu shot. Travelers can never be too prepared. That's the Hamacher philosophy. Don and Maggie guarantee that all the tired travelers will return home from a month in Egypt with happy smiles on their faces enriched by the wonders of the ancient world. Another remarkable trip shared with everyone through their eyes. We are grateful to them.

EGYPT - A JOURNEY THROUGH THE ACCIENT WORLD

THE SPHINX

THE GREAT PYRAMID
STEPS TO THE TUMB

EGYPTIAN MUSEUM

KING TUTANKHAMEN
(TUT)

MANY WALL PAINTINGS
IN BURIAL CHAMBERS

EGYPT - AN ADVENTURE

THE SEMIRAMIS INTER-CONTENTAL HOTEL

HORSE-DRAWN TAXI

ENJOYED LOTS OF SHOPPING

TAXI DRIVERS BARGAINING
WITH DON FOR HIRE.

21 DAY L;ION

THE NILE CRUISE WAS ANOTHER HIGH POINT

21 DAY LION

CHAPTER EIGHTEEN:
Once Upon a Water Mattress and the Latest Trips

In the summer of 2011 Maggie and Don, the fearless wayfarers, flew to California to try their hand at camping with their extended family.Yes, you guessed it—Yosemite National Park. The planning of such a venture was critical and came off like a charm. Their nephew, Howard Johnson, picked them up at the airport, and the adventure began with a visit to the wine country at Solbang, California. Don describes this town near Fresno as a quaint touristy place where wine tasting is the main attraction. They stayed overnight at the lovely Peterson Inn, a first class place where they enjoyed rooms in the garden area and a delicious formal breakfast. The high point of this first stop was watching the corral of Shetland ponies and several newborns just taking their first steps in the world. It was difficult for Don and Maggie to tear themselves away from this heartwarming sight, but it was time for the next step of the plan.

Their nephew handed them over to Robert Kuhn, a friend of their daughter Jeanine. His job was to drive them to Yosemite to meet up with the rest of the camping group. Don claimed the trip with Robert was extremely interesting because of the background of the driver. Robert Kuhn is a screenwriter who has written three movies including *The Cure* produced in 1995 and directed by Peter Horton, an accomplished actor. The movie centers on an eleven-year-old boy named Dexter who has AIDS. He befriends Eric, a slightly older boy with a violent mother. The cast includes Brad Renfro as Eric, Joseph Mazzello as Dexter, Diana Scaravid as Gail, and Annabella Sciorra as Linda. During the five hour drive to Yosemite, Robert had lively conversations with his passengers.

Barry Coker, Jeanine's husband, Jeni and Paul with their two sons, Hunter and Cameron, Lisa and her one year old son Asher, Loni (pregnant at the time and had to leave early) and husband Brad and their daughter Sienna made up the family gathering. Fortunately, Jeanine and Barry were the seasoned campers of the group and set up the camp for everyone's comfort. Diane was also scheduled to be there but had a work-related emergency. Don, the ninety year old patriarch and Maggie, the eighty-seven year old beauty queen matriarch, had a camping experience of a lifetime: one night sleeping in a tent on an air-filled mattress that took up the entire tent. Imagine crawling and walking on that surface in an attempt to get in and out of the shelter to answer nature's call in the middle of the night holding a flashlight. The good part of this experiment was hearing the rushing of the river nearby and/or imagining a bear liking your toes. The royal heads of the Hamacher clan spent the remaining nights at Yosemite in the beautiful, luxurious lodge. Their days were enjoyed eating at the campsite and seeing all the loveliness of the park, the falls, the Sequoia trees, Glacier Point in the presence of a devoted family. Relaxed and comfortable, the happy campers returned to the comfort of their home in South Carolina with the beauty of Yosemite, family and friends in their memories.

Fresh in their active minds as well is their recent annual jaunt to New York City where they stayed at the NY Quality Inn, saw *Chicago* and *C.S. Lewis' Letters* and took the night cruise around Manhattan. Maggie commented that seeing the lights of the Statue of Liberty and the Brooklyn Bridge at night is quite a treat for two people from Missouri.

This past year provided loads of marvelous moments on the road: the cruise on the Bahama Celebration when they won two prizes (free drinks) for being the oldest in the audience and for being married the longest. They flew to Austin, Texas to see Don's sister Frances who turned ninety-eight this year. Their fifty-first trip to the Kentucky Derby was another milestone.

The Hamacher 2011 travelogue is not over by any means. The fall foliage near Greenville calls them each year. On the way they stop at the favorite flea market in Pickens, South Carolina. They drive to Highlands, South Carolina and eat lunch in Cherokee, stay at the Pink Hotel and cookout there as usual. They admire the leaves at their loveliest at the Grandfather Mountain area near Boone, North Carolina and have the magnificent smorgas at the Daniel Boone Hotel. Don claims to be the the fourth great grand-son of Daniel Boone, pioneer from whom he probably inherited his fearlessness.

Don and Maggie are heading for Orlando and Fort Lauderdale for another September four day cruise. After that they drive to the August family reunion in Rochester, Michigan. They stay at the Hilton Hotel there but the activities are to be held at the home of Richard Bates, Don's sister Mary Agnes' son. Richard's family is known for loving fishing, hunting, and equestrian events. They expect about forty participants this year but as many as eighty-five have attended in the past when it was held in Gatlinburg.

We look forward to hearing about the fun they will have this year and years to come.

OUR CAMPING TRIP TO YOSEMINITE NATIONAL P[ARK

MAGGIE - AMAIZED AT ALL THE EQUIPMENT

BARRY'S COOKING IS GREAT

WE SLEPT IN THIS TENT

A HUGE SEQUOIA TREE

YOSEMINITE FALLS

CHAPTER NINETEEN

The Wise Women of the Hamacher Clan

Growing up with three sisters and four stepsisters often housed under one roof, clearly prepared Donald Hamacher for all challenges life would place before him. Pure survival as the single male amidst seven girls in the formative years might be labeled as miraculous. To the contrary the loving experience lead to great success and much happiness in adulthood. . Add one sharp wife, two accomplished daughters, four adoring granddaughters, several great granddaughters with more expected as of this writing, and two great grandsons who managed to slip into the Hamacher clan and the result is one very proud, contented gentleman.

Don's mother died when he was quite young and he remembers with love how his sisters divided up the job of taking care of him. Dorothy the oldest sister who died in her sixties was in his estimation a great achiever and technically the hardest working musician in the family. Don says, "She was valedictorian of her class, a gifted journalist, a piano soloist, an excellent mechanical musician, and a good organist."

"When Mother died," Don recalls, "They hired a maid but

Dorothy helped plan the meals. Frances mended and sewed clothes and made sure I always looked good. Mary Agnes had the assignment of playing with me and reading to me on a daily basis." Don adds that now Frances at age ninety-six plays lots of bridge at the senior center and is often asked to play the piano for songfests. On Fridays she goes to 'the Old Folks Home' to play for them. Mary Agnes he describes as a 'goer'. She loves concerts and attends one or more concerts a week at Kranard Hall at the university near her home. She plays at her church, her neighbor's church, a music club and recently participated in a dual piano presentation.

"Both Frances and Mary Agnes are fantastic." Don says proudly. "Both have what musicians call 'absolute ears' or perfect pitch. Just play a note and they know what it is. They are full of life, entertaining friends constantly. They can play anything and encourage their audiences to hum it and I'll play it. No musicians are as good as they are."

In return, Don's sisters recently sent their remembrances and impressions of him. On February 7, 2011 Frances wrote the following sentiments:

To Whom It May Concern:

So many memories run through my head that it is impossible to remember everything. We shared the same home until 1932 when I went off to college.

Interested in our own lives with friends, music lessons, etc. it did not occur to us that he, too, was talented. I don't know when he learned to play the clarinet. But he was absorbing music through osmosis all along.

In common we both had tonsils and adenoids removed at the same time. He was only four years old.

Daddy used to remind us to play a game or give some attention to our little motherless brother. We never had any arguments except insisting that he clean up after digging fortresses in the back yard with dog Fritz.

We all attended church regularly, often playing the hymns we liked on the piano at home. Ours was not a strict household except that Daddy frowned on Sunday movies.

Don was meanwhile excelling in Boy Scouts. I can't remember encouraging him or even sewing on a badge. I guess we three teen-aged girls were too self-interested.

It was good to hear that he had a scholarship to a school in Kansas. But then he transferred to the University of Missouri. I was a senior there and we met for lunch. I even washed two white shirts for him. (1939)

While teaching music in Alton, Illinois (1944), I heard a knock at the door. It was brother Donald, hitchhiking, with money hidden in his shoes! I wasn't aware of all his musical activities. Soon I was in the American Red Cross, first at Chanute Field and then overseas to England for nineteen months with 182nd General Hospital as a recreation worker.

"*Losing track of Don and Maggie I later learned of his great achievement with Musical Moods in Robinson, his success in Champaign High School and then with Dog N Suds. All along his musical genius was appearing.*

I was fortunate to arrange a couple tunes for four-part singing. I also like shortening sleeves; I even once made him a shirt. In common we both have two daughters each. I cannot say enough good things about our relationship and love for each other."

Frances Nelson
Don's older sister

Don's other sister, Mary Agnes, recently added the following comments about her brother's life:

My Impressions of my Brother, Don

"I could describe him as a happy, outgoing person, a real extravert— barring all health issues of his later years. He never knew a stranger! Thus, first impressions of him are as a pleasant, handsome, well-groomed guy. (Oh, how he loved clothes and wanted just the right mixes and matches of jackets, shirts, ties, etc. I really needed an extra closet when he came to visit just for the weekend.)

I would call him a perfectionist as I refer to music. Whether he is performing on the clarinet or saxophone or even singing in a choir, conducting or arranging the music or the score for a particular ensemble, it had to be just right! I've assisted him many times in his deciding the 'perfect cadence' or just a single chord-spelling to give the effect of a "German Diminished or an Italian 6th".

Occasionally he can be impetuous, but the situation is cleared up easily.

As a high school and college student Don always had positive and original goals. Whatever he was serious about (Examples: church, Boy Scouts, music, drum major), he pursued it with ardent determination. He showed his mathematical skills (no doubt inherited from his father) as he helped to work his way through college with various jobs—music, of course, in dance bands during the depression years.

Thus, going into the business world, he showed his excellent sense of organization, salesmanship, and financial acuity as is evidenced in the establishing of his successful Dog N Suds business.

Good as a leader, was President of the International Franchise Inc., etc—not sure here. In other words, I think Don loved to be up front. He wanted to be gregarious (very social). He loved people, made friends easily, was often spoken of as the life of the party. Also he could tell some great jokes (some a bit shady) but never offend—but continue to be a gentleman.

Don always showed his love of family, enjoyed organizing family reunions. Often times he was a procrastinator (like Findlay, who admits he was one).

A big hobby is genealogical records, pictures, etc. and creating many, many priceless scrapbooks.

Don had lots of original ideas for anything he did whether as a host for a party, the church or musical activity.

*Tell about your many kinds of programs: Musical Mood which was first of its kind; your jazz band musicals with that creative and original ability of yours!

I hope all this helps. I am trying to get this mailed today—Monday— so all my sentences aren't perfect—but—I tried to underline the main ideas and adjectives to describe you.

I didn't speak of your childhood. If needed you could say: "Big sister Mary Agnes did the most to take care of you: i.e. play games and read to you. You were always obedient and willing to do as I said!! Ha!!"

Mary Agnes
February 2011

The love and admiration that Don's sisters expressed are only a small sampling of the sentiments written by other members of his fan club. Maggie and Don have two daughters, Diane and Jeanine, whose comments give further insight into the real Hamacher world.

Of importance here is the commentary from the proud father about his daughters. Of Diane, the older, Don comments that she is an extravert and definitely concentrates on attainment with the goal of being able to live well in retirement. She is a very generous, caring person, dresses very well which adds to her natural beauty.

Earlier Diane worked for the Presbyterian Church as educational director. She now is in the teaching profession and has a job that her father would love to have. In Bay City, Michigan she places students into jobs in the community and is the liaison between the employers, the parents and the schools. He reports that Diane is well recognized in her community because of the vital service she provides for her special students and appreciative businesses. Diane's father added with fondness that she loves to dance, and has two wonderful daughters.

Diane's description of her father sheds light on the Hamacher persona from the first-born. She writes:

Some words that describe my dad:
Energetic—he liked to go morning, noon, and night.
Generous—always wanting to give what we needed
Likeable—had lots of friends
Detailed—explained every step of what he was thinking
Involved—active in community and social events
Organized—made lists and wanted to know what he was doing every day
Motivator—super salesman, could sell anything
Talkative—enjoyed telling jokes and stories
Musical—choir director for as long as I can remember

The stories that come to mind on a few days notice are:
1. *Detailed—I will never forget the four page, typewritten letter that Dad wrote to me on how to catch an airplane. Now, I was eighteen years old at the time as well as an A student. He spelled out every detail on how, where and when to park my car—how many steps to the terminal, how to stand in line to check in, what to say, what to do in the one hour plus wait that I would have...I wish I could find that letter (one of the few letters he wrote me).*
2. *Musical—When I was little, I remember Dad having the high*

school singers over to practice singing in trios and quartets. The students liked Dad and it was fun to listen and watch the practices.

3. Sunday was family day—we went to church and often joined another family (the Smiths) for lunch. They had two daughters the same age as my sister and me; and we all had a great time together. We also took some wonderful family vacations with the Smith family.

4. I will never forget one time when Mom and Dad came to visit me. I was divorced and my daughters were away at college. Dad and Mom helped me for one whole week with things around the house that needed to be fixed. At the end of the week, I felt terrible and cried because we had not done anything fun the entire week—only worked. Dad said that this had been one of the best visits with me because he felt needed and useful. That meant a lot to me."

Jeanine, the younger daughter, is a psychologist in the Salt Lake City, Utah schools. She has a doctorate and her proud father claims she scored 100's (not just A's) on all her tests. He describes Jeanine as a very caring person who deals with students with every problem in existence (drugs, pregnancy, family related). As a result of her efforts on their behalf, she receives letters from former students who claim she changed their lives for the better. Jeanine loves big dogs, mountain climbing, and is married to Barry Coker whom she met at an outdoorsman club. They realized they liked all the same things and have two daughters, Loni and Lisa.

Jeanine's essay about her dad exemplifies the level of respect his daughters feel for him:

My Dad

"My dad has always been there for me—to listen and help out whenever problems come my way. He has been generous with his time and money was never an object. He's a man of faith and Eagle Scout principles always trying to instill his beliefs in us kids. He is a man who always does what he says he is going to do and, boy, we better always do the same or we would hear about it. He is a man of his word! Dad has tons of energy. He would come home from a trip and wonder what the plan was for the next few days—filling every minute with projects, parties, bridge, golf, whatever. He still hasn't slowed down much to this day. He reminds me of that line in Rudyard Kipling's "IF"—"If you can fill the unforgiving minute with sixty seconds worth of distance run—yours is the earth and everything that's in it." Nothing ever stopped my dad. He always believed he could do anything and he has shared many wonderful experiences with his family from flying us to exciting places in his airplane to camping out in the beautiful outdoors. He is an amazing wonderful man and I am proud to call him my Dad!"

Editor's note: Obviously Don Hamacher's daughters adore him and cherish their family lives. This made me wonder what my own children would write about me! Scary thought.

The Granddaughters …

The first information that one must learn before hearing from the "Grands" is that they address their grandfather as Grandon. This is a most fitting title for the ultimate head of this devoted family. Needless to say, Diane's daughters, Jeni and Christie, and Jeanine's daughters, Loni and Lisa, dote on their Grandon. What a lucky fellow he is to have all these women loving him!

Jeni who is a medical doctor connected with Coastal Carolina University checks in with her Grandon daily. As Don puts it "She watches out for my heart valve problem". Don adds that Jeni was a doctor at the University of North Carolina for one year while her husband worked on a research project at Duke. From North Carolina they moved to the Myrtle Beach area and raised their children in close contact with Maggie and Don. Jeni's husband is a member of theWaccamaw Radiologists Group. Of her grandfather Jeni writes:

I would describe Grandon as a persistent go-getter who has always been able to get what he wanted. When he met my grandma, apparently, he wanted to go out with her. She wanted nothing to do with him. He was persistent and exasperated. She finally told him that if he saw after class, he could take her out. In an attempt to avoid him, she took the back exit from the building that her class was in, however, of course, he was waiting for her.

He is also filled with energy. When I was a teenager, we would come to Myrtle Beach to visit and he would have an hour-by-hour calendar of things to do. We would pack in miniature golf, beach trips, shopping, meals, and movies. I would be exhausted and he would still have the energy to go.

Grandon always seemed to have a positive outlook, no matter what the situation might be.

Grandon has always been very mathematical. He is able to add large numbers in his head.

Grandon has always been a joker, always telling jokes, especially shady ones.

Jennifer

Diane's second daughter Christie graduated from Alma College with a bachelor's degree in business and sociology She has followed in her grandfather's footsteps with a successful career in sales. She is married to Ryan Randolph, a residential builder and avid fly fisherman. They have two darling daughters, Taylor Elizabeth and Peyton Riley. Christie writes:

Hi, Grandon,

"I'm very excited to read the book that you're working on. I think it's a fabulous idea. Something we'll have for many generations to come.

Key words that describe you:

☐ *Persistent*
☐ *High energy*
☐ *Social*
☐ *Center of attention*
☐ *Entertaining*
☐ *Salesman*
☐ *Creative*
☐ *Entrepreneurial*
☐ *Dramatic*
☐ *Critical*

A few memories that I have:

Of course there are many memories on Holloway Circle; going to the ocean, devotions in the chairs out front, walking to the surf, ice cream at the neighbors next door (Gladys), all of us playing rummy-kum...the list is endless.

You and my father took me to the Par 3 golf course where I played my first game of real golf. It was very exciting for me as I remember playing better than both of you on certain holes...beginner's luck!

I remember traveling around in your plane with Grandmaggie and Jennifer, my sister. My memories are a very small backseat, weighing our luggage and vomiting all over Jennifer.

I have very fond memories of crabbing. I remember driving to Cherry Grove to get the disgusting flounder heads from the very smelly fish shop. From there, we traveled to the marina where your boat' Is She Gonna' was docked. We all piled in the back of the boat to start our day in the sun of crabbing. After hours in the sun, alligators swimming and an unreliable *boat, we'd have excellent lunches packed by Grandmaggie. That evening, I remember too the tortuous screaming of the Crabs in the boiling water and their occasionally getting out of the pot and our frantic chase in the kitchen to capture them. With newspaper layered all over the kitchen table, the eating soon began. Too much work for so little meat, but excellent tasting nonetheless. After 2-3 more hours at the dinner table, we'd finish the day's catch.*

It wasn't many years ago that the Surf Club was soliciting bids for new flatware and furniture for their remodel. It still makes me smile when I think of you inquiring about the flatware they were interested in and asking if you could submit a proposal. They said sure; I'm sure all the while thinking what is this 80 year old man going to submit. Hours of internet research and pricing, you created your proposal, submitted it and had it accepted. Maybe one of your last big sales projects, but always the salesman at heart.

I have many more memories of course. Your life has been very successful and filled with positive memories. I'm proud to say you're my grandfather."

With love,
Christie

Loni, Jeanine's first daughter, recently earned a Ph.D. in psychology from the University of Utah. She enjoys the same profession as her mother, helping kids in trouble. Loni is married to a builder and they have a daughter, Siena and a son, Dekin. Her view of her grandfather is truly touching. She sent on the following letter to her grandfather:

About Grandon—

The first thing that comes to mind when I think of my grandfather is his love for adventure. He has traveled around the world and visited more places than anyone I know. From African safaris to sailing a rented boat around in the Caribbean, no adventure seemed too extreme. I remember flying with him in his airplane and his seemingly calm demeanor when he announced we may not make it this time. We also visited several national parks together. Grandon was extremely organized and planned everything down to the smallest detail for every trip we took; from what we would eat for every meal including the condiments we would use to all the activities we would do every day. We had a lot of fun together on all our family trips.

Another talent known by all is his excellent musical ability. I will always remember him playing the saxophone at family gatherings and at church. I will remember how he directed the choir for so many years. His musical talent is truly remarkable.

Not to be forgotten is his ability to shop for a bargain. When I was a child, he would give me ten dollars for every birthday. Then he would spend hours helping me figure out the best way to spend it and what I could get for that amount of money. We would go around to every store in town, compare prices, and take notes on which store had the cheapest prices. We would always get the best deal."

Your loving granddaughter,
Loni

According to Don, Jeanine's other daughter, Lisa, is married to a psychologist and both are working on their doctorates. His admiration for her adventurous spirit shows in his description of Lisa's nature and travels. He claims "she is kind of a loner who went to Nepal on her own, stayed in hostels, then eventually got a job teaching English there. When she returned she became a firefighter in Colorado. She traveled to Brazil at some point." He added that Lisa did not like to have her picture taken but is getting over that. Don felt that she did not like to be in the limelight.

Lisa titled her account **Grandon**

She writes:

Grand-Don is a person with the tenacity and drive to make things happen. He has never been one to waste time dreaming when he could be planning. In fact, planning a constant stream of creative ventures and adventures to embark on seems to be Grand-Don's favorite pastime. The summertime trips we took when I was a child, flawlessly planned by Grand-Don, were full of great memories and every moment was action-packed. I remember the picnics in the parks and elaborate meals cooked in motel rooms. I remember beautiful scenery and great conversation. Being 'on-the-road' with Grand-Don was always a great experience.

Grand-Don's organizational skills have always been an inspiration to me. Every time he came to visit my family, he would organize a different part of the house: the garage, the basement, the kitchen, etc. He always did an amazing job and was appreciated.

Always excited about each new day and taking on any challenges with an air of remarkable confidence, Grand-Don is, without a doubt, a happy man. His crafty manner and enthusiasm make him fun to be around and he often is the life of the party. I am truly proud to be his granddaughter.

Lisa

OUR FAMILY OF GIRLS

LISA - MARGARET - LONI
JEANINE - CHRISTIE - JENI DIANE

CHAPTER TWENTY:
The Way I Look at Life

Do not avoid reading this important part of the life and times of Don Hamacher. We elder statesmen are well aware of the effect our so-called wise words have on the needy younger generation. Lots of eye rolling, ear plugging, vacant staring into space, and text messaging occur when we-who-lived-a-long-and-full-life attempt to teach youngsters valuable lessons. Let it be known that these reactions do not discourage Don Hamacher from stating his well-earned philosophy on who he is at the glorious age of ninety-one. So sit back and think about what he places before you.

My attitude is ME. It is who I am. Maya Angelou said it best: When a person shows you who he is—believe him. A positive outlook controls my thinking at all times. I have always looked forward, never backward. As a result, I have always enjoyed the most important things in life: a loving marriage and family, a successful career and business, exciting adventures, devoted friends, and unlimited happiness. Don't get me wrong. I have made mistakes along the way but have refused to dwell on those misjudgments. Instead I tried to correct errors when possible and then put all my efforts toward a better future. I realize that one does not constantly have to be the winner but must be able to say, "I have done my very best".

I do harbor some regrets that Maggie and I have discussed. I feel that I have not volunteered enough and now at my age I am bothered that I cannot do more for my church and the community. I do substitute for Meals on Wheels and when called upon, I truly receive more satisfaction than the appreciative people I serve. My service to the church choirs has warmed my heart for many, many years. I am grateful for those opportunities. I have been blessed.

The most important miracle in my life is Maggie. I have not only loved my wife but I have always appreciated her beauty both inwardly and outwardly. She has been a great inspiration for me and I have always been proud to be her spouse. Maggie has always been a queen everywhere she has been. Crowned in her freshman and junior years in college she was even elected the queen at her 50th class reunion. She has been and forever will be the royalty in our family. Everyone loves Maggie, most especially, her husband of sixty-eight years.

Maggie and I begin the day together with morning devotions that keep us close to each other and our religion. We have established a personal relationship with our Lord, thanking Him for our blessings. I have learned to pray and talk to Him and have become aware of the true meaning of religion passed down to me by my father's example in my youth.

For many years I have kept a paragraph entitled "Attitude Is Everything" written by Charles Swindoll that clearly describes the foundation of my thinking:

"The longer I live, the more I realize the impact of attitude on life. Attitude, to me, is more important than facts. It is more important than the past, than education, than money, than circumstances, than failures, than successes, than what other people think or say or do. It is more important than appearance, than giftedness or skill. It will make or break a company...a church...a home. The remarkable thing is, we have a choice every day regarding the attitude we will embrace for the day. We cannot change our past. We cannot change the fact that people act a certain way. We cannot change the inevitable. The only thing we can do is play the one string we have, and that is our attitude. I am convinced that life is 10% what happens to you and 90% of how you react to it. And so it is with all of us. We are in charge of our own attitudes."

Add to that Anne Frank's words "I don't think of all the misery but the beauty that still remains." "It's all in the attitude.

I am so thankful that I have lived such a happy and eventful life."

Donald Hamacher
April 2011

CHAPTER TWENTY-ONE:
The Final Thoughts... An Epilogue

Of these conditions I am sure: that each member of my family, every friend that I have left, my friendly UPS driver and my favorite checker at Kroger are in a state of pure relief for the first time this Year of our Lord 2012. They will no longer see the faraway expression on my face, that annoying stare of distraction caused by the constant feeling that I should be home alone sitting in front of my computer, writing and thus completing the memoirs of a spectacular ninety-one-year old gentleman. My inner circle of family and friends was weary of my blank look indicating that my mind was elsewhere. After all, I had agreed to attempt this awesome mission and had spent months (really a year) interviewing, listening, taking notes, transcribing those scribbles, translating thoughts, rethinking, correcting, revising, rewriting, adding and subtracting, and driving to North Myrtle Beach from my Murrells Inlet home in supposedly laid-back South Carolina. . Twenty-one segments later and a mere 27,000 words (give or take) should really be enough to cover the wonder of this marvelous lifespan and to reduce my anxiety level. Hopefully, this story of an honorable man, his amazing wife, and his incredible family serves as a perfect plan for readers interested in how to live a long, valuable life.

The task has not been easy for this writer. Listening with clear understanding and relating with sincere empathy to others are not my strongest assets. There are many moments in my life when I have had to force myself to care about the accomplishments and thoughts of others. I realize this is a serious shortcoming on my part and I am learning to deal with it. One effective tool I use is to recall repeatedly the words of Bill Moyers, the brilliant PBS commentator and philosopher, who once said that if he had not had children he would not have learned to love anyone other than himself. This bit of wisdom helped to keep my focus on Don Hamacher at ninety-one years of age, not the rigors of writing his story. The process of completing this assignment was comparable to having a child. Laborious, but amazing. This aided in documenting his story with integrity.

By today's standards Don's life may be labeled as "uncool" or "too good to be true".In truth it is a life filled with championing the necessity of boy scouting, religious devotion, loving family ties, business assertiveness, musical talent, leadership, and unselfish community service. How straight-laced this lifestyle may seem in our overly sophisticated technical world. On the contrary, this writer has learned quite a lesson from this stellar example of "good clean living". The story is filled with great fun, daring feats, risk taking, extensive travel, countless adventures. Everyone should be so fortunate to experience such fulfillment in our brief stay on earth.

Not to be missed are the delightful writings contributed by the subject's older sisters, his children, and grandchildren. Their words are golden. I enjoyed their descriptions and stories about my subject; especially the keen insight from Don's older sisters who are loving life in their mid-nineties. I can only imagine how beautiful they are.

The real reward of this experience is the privilege of observing the respect evident between these life partners of sixty-eight years and counting and that life is never over when one leaves a legacy honored forever by those who follow. The message was never "Well, when I was your age I did things the right way." In truth, the lesson learned is "This is the way I chose to live; follow my lead and you will be as happy as I am."

Gail Ritrievi
May 2012